Unfolding Our New Humanity

Sukie Colegrave

Dedicated to my granddaughter, Sophia Moorehead and the rest of us as we unfold our true nature.

ACKNOWLEDGMENTS

With love and gratitude to each of my teachers, in form and formlessness; to Dorothy Luciano for her tireless, caring and insightful editing; to Forest for her perceptive and detailed reflections; to my daughter, Laura, a beloved friend; to Bob Vogelsang for his caring, patient, technical help; and to Yugharli.

Also by Sukie Colegrave

- Uniting Heaven and Earth
- By Way of Pain: a Passage into Self
- Embodying the Light of Oneness

TABLE OF CONTENTS

INTRODUCTION

The seed of the new human is latent within each of us. While the archetypal nature of the unfolding of this seed is common to us all, the experience of this unfolding is unique for each of us, occurring at different times, in different ways, and by way of different life experiences.

Just as the seed of the new human unfolds naturally by way of a series of transformative passages, so the structure of this book reflects and explores these passages. Attending first to the unfolding of the new human mind and heart, the book moves on to explore the ultimate passages of the realization of our new humanity - the unfolding of our new human body. Once the essential nature of the new human Being, mind, heart and body, has been unveiled, the book concludes with an exploration of the new human life spontaneously lived by the new human Being and, ultimately, the new humanity.

Each of the key passages of the book concludes with a guided meditation designed to facilitate direct experience of each passage of unfolding and thereby prepare the reader for the following passage.

Woven into the conceptual content of the passages of transformation are some personal experiences. These are included to reveal some of the experiences that birthed this book. As well as to complement the more transpersonal nature of the discussion with the vitality and warmth inherent in individual experience. They are just brief examples of one person's experience of certain moments and passages of unfolding. They are not intended as a complete autobiography. Nor are they intended to suggest that others might experience their own unfolding in similar ways.

When you read this book fully present not just in your mind, but also in your heart and body, you may find the spirit of the book more accessible than if you rely on conceptual comprehension alone. For intellect disconnected from heart is one of the salient characteristics of the old human consciousness of separation, the consciousness that creates and perpetuates the dark night of pain and suffering. At best, intellect alone reveals the part and misses the whole that we are. It misses the Light, Love and Life of our true nature - One Being expressing as infinite diversity.[1] It misses the aliveness of truth.

If the spirit of the words that follow resonate with you, quickening your innate sense of truth about the nature of who we are, then they are useful. If they quicken sacred questions whose presence, honored with devotion, invite answers that unfold consciousness, then they are also useful. If they offer neither of these or any other gifts to you, then, trusting they are not for you, at least for now, please gently put this book aside. Since this book is simply an offering to those whose hearts resonate with it. It is not written to convince or

---

[1] Throughout this book, I use the word "Light" to suggest Divine Being, Source of all that is. I am not referring to white light, but, rather, to our Divine nature, Light of I Am, that is the source of all colors including white light.

persuade. It is offered only because the experiences and the principal practice for embodying Being it describes were offered to me to embody and share.

*Throughout this book, I use the word "Light" to suggest Divine Being, Source of all that is. I am not referring to white light, but, rather, to our Divine nature, Light of I Am, that is the source of all colors including white light.

Unfolding the experience of reading with the union of mind, heart and body.

1. Allow your awareness to rest in your brain.

2. Allow your awareness and brain together to read a paragraph from this chapter.

3. Allow your awareness to extend down into your chest and heart area, and on down into your legs, so that your awareness now includes both your head, heart and your whole body.

4. Now, with the field of awareness including both your head, heart and body, read the same paragraph. Allow yourself not only to conceptually understand the sentences but also to feel the energy of what is being communicated.

5. Notice whether or not your heart resonates with the message of the paragraph.

From my heart to yours, heart of Being.

I listen with a silence we rarely hear;
a peace that grows our bones.
I live as us
when we believe we live alone,
and hold our hand
when we feel that I have fled.
I sing to us in the blindfold of the night;
and carry us across the desert sea.

We may believe that I have turned away;
but only we can make that turn.
We may believe my breasts no longer flow with milk;
but only we can cease to drink.
We may believe my heart no longer loves;
but only we can bolt the door.

I cannot turn away from us, for we are I.
I cannot cease to love these hearts of mine.
But we can turn away and cease to feel
my touch,
my breath.

Or we can turn and see my face,
and drink the waters of my life.
We can open to my heart
as the essence of our own.

And know us as apple tree
and song that births the apple seed.

PASSAGE 1

An Offering

A group of blind men heard that a strange animal, called an elephant, had been brought to the town, but none of them were aware of its shape and form. Out of curiosity, they said: "We must inspect and know it by touch, of which we are capable". So, they sought it out, and when they found it they groped about it. In the case of the first person, whose hand landed on the trunk, said, "This being is like a thick snake". For another one whose hand reached its ear, it seemed like a kind of fan. As for another person, whose hand was upon its leg, said, the elephant is a pillar-like a tree-trunk. The blind man who placed his hand upon its side said, "elephant is a wall". Another who felt its tail described it as a rope. The last felt its tusk, stating the elephant is that which is hard, smooth and like a spear. **Wikipedia**

I n this ancient Indian parable, the elephant symbolizes the ultimate reality of who we are. The blind men are us humans, our eyes veiled by the limitations of our consciousness. When we touch or glimpse the one reality that we are, we may believe we have awoken to the one whole, absolute reality of our Divine nature. Whereas, more often, we are merely beginning to awake and are confusing our embryonic experience and understanding with complete realization.

When we humbly acknowledge ourselves as the blind men encountering the elephant, we quicken within an eagerness to honor and open to each other's experiences and perspectives, and, thereby, unfold into consciousness more of the wholeness that we are - one Divine Presence expressing through each unique individual humanity.

Our current human nature is not, as many of us have been conditioned to believe, complete. We are not a finished product, fundamentally unchanging and unchangeable. We are not limited by a narrow spectrum of consciousness, from fear to compassion, circumscribed within the experience of separation from each other and all existence. Nor are we subject to inevitable disease and death. However, since this experience of ourselves as isolated identities separate from all existence, and suffering the pain inherent in separate consciousness has not changed significantly in recorded history, many of us have assumed that this is all that we are.

Many of us have forgotten that there is, in truth, only One Being expressing as all that is, as all experience. We have forgotten the absolute wellbeing, peace, wholeness, bliss, omniscience, omnipresence, creativity, unconditional Love and immortal Life of our original Divine nature. We have forgotten that while we may experience an individual unfolding of consciousness, a unique journey of forgetting and remembering, our essential nature is always and only One Divine Presence expressing its Self as many faces; experiencing its Self as many different levels of consciousness including and transcending the experience of separation.

Our fall into the darkness of separation and suffering continued for so many thousands of years that many of us assumed that, even if separation and suffering are not all that we are, they are all we are able to know. We forgot that our belief in a relatively unchanging human nature was merely an expression of the dark night of human consciousness, our "fall" into the experience of separation and suffering rather than the truth of who we are. We forgot that who we consider ourselves to be as well as who we have perceived ourselves to be since the inception of recorded history, merely reflects one level of consciousness, one way of experiencing existence.

However, these days more and more of us are beginning to stir from our long night of forgetfulness. New Light is quickening our awareness. New seeds of remembering are unfolding within our hearts. From the dark night of separation and suffering increasing numbers of us are not only intuiting the Oneness of all existence but, jolted by the pain of political, economic, ecological and psychological conflict, beginning, at least momentarily, to glimpse our original nature - One Divine Being.[2]

Awakening out of the sleep of separation, instead of being a one-time event, is a gradual unveiling and unfolding of who we are. Just as our experience of awakening each morning out of sleep into our human body is different when we are a child

---

[2] To clarify, I am capitalizing the Divine and all synonyms for the Divine, like Being, Light, Oneness, Love, etc. Since all that is, all existence is Divine, distinguishing between the Divine and relative experiences and expressions of Divine, like, for example, light and dark, is, of course, untrue. However, in the interests of clarity, it can be useful to distinguish between Divine consciousness awake to its Divine nature and other levels of consciousness, like the experience of duality, that still sleep to their Divine nature.

than when we are an adult, so too our experience of awakening out of the sleep of separate consciousness differs as our consciousness refines, unfolds and elevates.

Awakening into who we are spontaneously initiates a process of embodying who we are at each level of our humanity - mind, heart and, ultimately, biology. It is this unfolding of our true nature at each level of our humanity, this embodying of more and more of our Divine nature, that allows us not only to know and realize who we are, but increasingly to live and express the Divine that we are as unique human beings living unique human lives on our greater body, the Earth.

This book explores our true human nature and offers a simple way of awakening, unfolding and embodying it in mind, heart and body. A way suited to this time. It explores the four unfoldings of consciousness that unfold the new Divine human nature. The first unfolding is our original incarnation, as a spark of Divine Presence, Light of Being, into and as an individual human being on our greater body, the Earth. The second unfolding is our awakening out of the experience of separation (*Passage* 3), out of identification with any experience, mental, emotional or sensory, into our true nature, one Light of Being (Oneness) expressing as infinite diverse experiences. The third unfolding is the embodying of Light/Love/Life of Being in mind, heart and body (*Passages* 5 - 7), while the fourth unfolding completes the embodiment of Being, allowing the dissolution of mortal, biological body into Divine Body/ immortal Body of Light (*Passages* 8 and 9). This book focuses on the second, third and fourth unfoldings of human consciousness.

We may not hear much about the new awakening, the new unfolding and embodying of our essential Divine nature, in our schools, universities, and offices. We rarely hear about it in mainstream media, since much of our educational, political, economic, social and even medical systems are controlled by those in the thrall of the darkness of separate consciousness and, therefore perpetuating our experience of ourselves as isolated individuals. For this psychic darkness, infusing many of our ruling elites, knows we can more easily be controlled and manipulated while we remain weakened by the experience of conflict, lack, fear, disease, and ignorance inherent in separate consciousness; while we live disempowered, believing separation to be not only who we are, but, essentially, who we always were and always will be. This darkness knows we can be more easily exploited and abused while we believe we are dependent on others for wisdom, love, wellbeing, guidance and health.

Our escalating technological creativity, arising in part from the dark night of human consciousness, from the experience of separation and suffering, provides us with technological substitutes for the Divine creativity and absolute wellbeing we have forgotten we are. Its increasing power offers us two choices. On the one hand, we can become addicted to its apparent gifts and opportunities, allowing ourselves to be seduced and supported by sophisticated technological crutches as we walk deeper into forgetting our Divine nature. We can become increasingly dependent on what technology appears to provide, and, thereby, perpetuate our experience of separation, ignorance, impotence and pain.

On the other hand, we can walk a different way. With discernment, we can appreciate and use some of this new technology, selecting from the technological smorgasbord those technologies that authentically serve us as we awaken and embody our original Divine nature. We can use these new technologies, grateful for their ephemeral support, recognizing them for what they are - mere reflections of our forgotten, dormant, inner technologies, reflections of our Divine power, creativity and wisdom. For example, we can surf the web while, simultaneously, recognizing the internet as a reflection of the omniscience that is our essential nature, and allow this mirror of our omniscience to inspire and quicken our dedication to awakening out of our sleep of ignorance into Divine omniscience.

While there is only one Being, only one Divine presence, there are many ways and experiences of awakening as and embodying Being, as well as many ways of communicating our awakening and embodying of Being. There are many ancient spiritual traditions, many different psycho/spiritual practices, rituals and ceremonies that offer authentic, effective ways to facilitate the unfolding of our Divine nature. There are also new, simple ways of unfolding, appropriate for this time of accelerated transformation of consciousness. The way shared in this book is only one path of embodied unfolding. It is a way that only serves those for whom it is right, and is irrelevant to those more suited to other paths. It is a way for our time, not only because it embraces our busy life experiences into the cauldron of our metamorphosis, but also because it is a way arising from and reflective of the subtler energies, the higher consciousness currently enveloping the solar system. Moreover, as we shall see, it is a way that not only unfolds the new Divine human but is itself the nature of the new Divine human.

When we listen to and trust the inclinations and quiet promptings of the heart and body, rather than our emotional compulsions and fears and our mental oughts and shoulds, the still voice of our heart and body leads us home. It leads us along the path that is most graceful, effective and harmonious for each of us, regardless of how different this path may appear to be to the paths of friends, family and colleagues. While we may honor and respect our spiritual teachers, we need to remember our ultimate teacher and teaching lies only within the Divine essence of who we are.

Before reading further into this book, it may serve to ask yourself whether you are authentically open to the possibility that human nature could radically and fundamentally change; whether you are open to the possibility that who we humans have considered and experienced ourselves to be for thousands of years may not be who we are. If, as you ask these questions, you notice fears, judgments, and other mental and emotional resistances arising within yourself in response to the question you could simply allow and accept these reactions to be just the way they are, for as long as they are. If it feels appropriate, you could also allow awareness to drop into silence beneath this emotional and mental noise, and ask silence of Being these same questions.

PASSAGE 2

Invitation into the New Humanity

When I was in my twenties I dreamt of a man whom I had met a few times.

As I am present with this dream man, undisturbed by emotions or thoughts, I experience his body dissolving into a brilliant "star" of clear Light/Love and immortal Life. My body also dissolves into an identical "star" of clear Light/Love/Life. As this happens our male and female natures remember their wholeness, their androgyny. Like two flames close to each other, we ignite into one flame. Our one flame of Being spontaneously awakes as Source of all experience, Light/Love/Life of Being, Light of I Am, Divine Oneness.[3]

---

[3] In this book I usually refer to Creative Source, Divine consciousness, the One Divine Being that we are as Light of Being since the early dreams, visions and experiences that birthed this book portrayed our true nature as the one, clear "Light" expressing as different levels of consciousness, Divine Light expressing as all experience, as all that is.

However, as many ancient spiritual traditions, including the ancient Daoists, acknowledge, the Dao that can be named is not the eternal Dao. For any name implies that the thing named is not something else. Whereas, in truth, our true nature is all and everything. It is Source and all expressions and experiences of Source. Therefore, our original Divine

As Light of Being, I Am home. I Am whole – limitless, eternal potential. I Am Light/Love and immortal Life. I am Divine Presence expressing as all that is, as all levels of consciousness and experience - mineral, plant, animal, human, galactic, cosmic and transcendent. I Am One and the many unique faces of One. I Am bliss of Being doing nothing, being no one, going nowhere.

"Now that you are awakening out of the illusion of separation into our true Divine nature," says the one Light that we are in the wordless language of Light, "You need to return to Earth. As a human, you need to embody Light, Love and immortal Life of Being. You need to allow our true nature, Light of Being, to shine as your human mind, heart and body and, with human language, you need to share the living language of Light - the truth of Being."

Light of Being that I Am begins descending towards the familiar density of Earth and densifying into my human individuality.

Standing at the threshold of the human and Earthly world, I witness the condensation of Light of Being, of Divine consciousness, into the sense-perceptible experience. I understand that it is this condensation of Light of Being that gives rise to the experience of separation and suffering. My young human heart is shocked by the conflict and pain permeating human life - conflict between mind and heart, male and female, tribe and nation, as well as between much of humanity and the Earth. I am stunned by the degree of social, economic, biological, personal and environmental disharmony reflective of our experience of separation from each other, -the Earth and our true nature, Light of Being.

---

nature is nameless. Any name we use, at best, points to who we are. Since some of us find our hearts resonating more with one name than another, I use here a number of different names to point to our true nature. As well as Light of Being, I refer to our Divine nature as "Oneness", "Divine consciousness", "Light of I Am".

Human languages taste like ashen husks of truth, energetically divorced from the living language of Light. Depleted concepts disconnected from who we are - Light/Love/Life of Being.

At the time I received this dream I had not heard of anything called the language of Light. I was living in London, working on my doctorate, mothering my beloved six-year-old daughter, and dedicating much of my available free time to psycho/spiritual healing and unfolding.

The dream was a gift that goes on giving, both for me and for collective consciousness - a dream for this time of human awakening. A dream for those of us whose heart feels called to relinquish the experience of separation and suffering, and unfold and embody our Divine nature - Light of Being; both an invitation and revelation of the new human, the new humanity. Each time I feel I have received all its gifts, it unfolds deeper insights and experience. Like an icon it energetically allows consciousness to move through its living images into subtler experiences of the imageless Light of Being that we are.

Regardless of whether we are awake as the One Being that we are, or sleeping as separate consciousness, whether we know it or not, we are eternally Light of Being, Divine consciousness expressing as all experience; and therefore including and transcending all polarity, such as male and female, light and dark, spirit and matter.

We may call our essential nature, Divine consciousness, Light of Being, the original creative sound, Source, the Word, Life, Love, God, the Dao, or any number of words that different cultures and spiritual traditions use to name our un-nameable, essential nature. I use "Light" in this book because this is how our original nature first unveiled itself in my early dreams, visions, and awakening experiences. I also use "Light" as at this time we humans are awakening from seemingly darker, denser states of consciousness into lighter, subtler ones. We are awakening from the sleep of separate consciousness into the Light of unity consciousness, into the radiance of our original nature, Divine consciousness. We are enlightening and, in time, our human mind, heart and body are embodying and, thereby, living our enlightening.[4]

With the succinctness of image, the dream reveals that while who we are - Divine, Light of Being - is eternal, indivisible and unchanging, Light of Being simultaneously expresses as the differentiation, diversity and change that characterize human experience. The dream reveals matter as simply energy, as consciousness expressing as different forms and condensations.

As each of us awaken from the long, painful night of separate consciousness into our true nature, one Light of

---

[4] In this book I usually refer to Creative Source, Divine consciousness, the One Divine Being that we are as Light of Being since the early dreams, visions and experiences that birthed this book portrayed our true nature as the one, clear "Light" expressing as different levels of consciousness, Divine Light expressing as all experience, as all that is.

However, as many ancient spiritual traditions, including the ancient Daoists, acknowledge, the Dao that can be named is not the eternal Dao. For any name implies that the thing named is not something else. Whereas, in truth, our true nature is all and everything. It is Source and all expressions and experiences of Source. Therefore, our original Divine nature is nameless. Any name we use, at best, points to who we are. Since some of us find our hearts resonating more with one name than another, I use here a number of different names to point to our true nature. As well as Light of Being, I refer to our Divine nature as "Oneness", "Divine consciousness", "Light of I Am".

Being, each of us does so in our unique way. In this life, my first remembering of who we are arrived when I was about eighteen months old. I was sitting in a baby carriage looking at my twin brother sitting opposite me. He and I were inseparable from our cozy time in our mother's womb. Life felt safe, warm and suffused with love as long as we were together, which, at that time, was almost always.

On this particular day, it was raining. So both hoods of the twin baby carriage were pulled up forming a small, dark room on wheels. I remember the comforting sound of the soft rain landing on the hood of the baby carriage as it was being pushed down the country lane leading to the nearby village.

I looked across our little, safe space on wheels at my twin brother, enjoying our closeness. Suddenly, the proverbial light bulb flashed on and I experienced pre-conceptually that there is only one of us, only one Being expressing as all existence, including the little boy and girl sitting opposite each other in the baby carriage. Simultaneously, I awoke to the paradox of our Divine nature. For just as I experienced only one of us, one Being, I simultaneously experienced the unique individuality of each human expression of Being, including, of course, my brother and myself.

Although this timeless glimpse of our true nature, Divine Oneness, rapidly faded from consciousness, this early awakening in the baby carriage unconsciously guided and unfolded the subsequent passages of my life. Like a light in the darkness, it beckoned me home out of the darkness of pain, ignorance and suffering. It birthed an ineradicable knowledge that collectively we humans are now ready to unfold more of our true nature, and, thereby, birth a new world reflective of our Divine nature. In different ways during different passages of my life, it seeded experiences and interests that initiated and nurtured the unfolding and embodying of who we are.

One evening, when my twin brother and I were about twelve, our mother drove us to a friend's birthday party. The first thing I saw as I walked into our friend's house were three boys wearing long-haired brown wigs, which someone told me were Beatles' wigs. I had never before seen long hair on boys. My heart instantly lit up at the sight of these wigs. I knew intuitively they symbolized the dawning of a new era for humanity, the awakening of human consciousness from its long sleep.

The next catalyst of my awakening occurred when I was sixteen and I fell in love with a man, many years older than I, who produced documentaries for the BBC. At the time I met him he was making films about the depth psychologist, C.G. Jung and the Austrian spiritual teacher, Rudolf Steiner. Exploring the work of these two men not only facilitated occasional experiences of the Oneness that I had first glimpsed in the baby carriage, but also provided me with practices for unfolding the wellbeing of our Oneness.

I began opening in meditation to the blissful equanimity of Being accessible between our thoughts, emotions, images and sensations. As I did so, I became increasingly aware of my tendency to deny or mentally process uncomfortable perceptions to avoid experiencing them. I recognized well-rehearsed habits of analyzing, conceptualizing and storying pain rather than allowing my heart simply and unconditionally to accept each painful experience just the way it is. Gradually, by way of many, long forgettings and occasional rememberings, I learned that when we unconditionally accept the pain of yearning and fear just as it is, rather than being overwhelmed by it or attempting to figure it out and fix it, a space in the heart unfolds allowing intelligent, loving response to pain instead of emotional reaction and, thereby, more pain for ourself and others.

I was humbled by C.G. Jung's perspective of our "shadow" as including both our unconscious negative attitudes and psychological wounds as well as our unconscious Divine, benevolent qualities. With the help of my dreams and a wise and compassionate Jungian analyst, I began to acknowledge and accept my dark side, including my propensity to protect myself from emotional pain by projecting my "darkness" onto others. I began, for example, to acknowledge my tendencies to judge others for my perception of their fear, coldness, narcissism and arrogance rather than recognizing these qualities in myself. I noticed how quickly I "saw" and judged the splinter in another's eye rather than acknowledging the beam in my own. I became aware that as my heart accepted into consciousness my own dark thoughts, emotions and behaviors it became easier to access and accept the psychological wounds at the root of these dark mental, emotional and behavioral habits. I noticed the flame of unconditional acceptance beginning to heal these buried wounds, and, thereby, spontaneously unveiling more regular experiences of our Divine nature such as peace and unconditional Love.

My heart, hitherto largely veiled by the contraction of fear and the incessant clamor of insatiable desires, began more often to experience its true nature - one Divine heart of intelligent, unconditional Love. Yet despite this growing awareness of the bliss, Love and peace of Being, identification with emotional desires, attachments, my physical body as well as chronic monkey mind regularly hijacked my consciousness, collapsing it back once more into the pain of separate consciousness.

It was not until I was in my early thirties that a sudden three day awakening into our true Divine identity, Light of Being, highlighted that regular, lengthy imprisonments in the pain of separation were no longer necessary. It not only reminded me of the ever-present invitation of relinquishing forever the experience of separation and suffering by unfolding our Divine nature, Light of I AM, but emphasized the potential for this death of separate consciousness and rebirth into unity consciousness existed for many of us.

I was with my new husband, honeymooning in Spain. We were in the city of Avila, sacred to me due to its association with the medieval Christian mystics, St. John of the Cross and St. Theresa.

During the month leading up to our honeymoon, I had been aware of increasing pressure on the crown of my head. Daily it seemed as though an immense presence was pressing on the top of my head, waiting for my permission to flow down through my scalp and permeate my whole body. While I didn't understand this presence, I trusted its benevolence. I felt interested, excited and inspired by it. While initially, I did not relate this benevolent presence above my head to who we are, Light of Being, the experience frequently reminded me of a small postcard given to me by the comparative religion teacher at my English boarding school. The postcard was a photo of Holman Hunt's painting of Christ knocking at the door.

Holman Hunt
Light of the World

Although I had never particularly enjoyed the painting, I kept the postcard with me because I was inspired by the words from the New Testament that my religion teacher had written for me beneath the photo:

"Behold, I stand at the door and knock: if any man hear my voice, and open the door, I will come into him, and will sup with him, and he with me." Revelations 3:20.

My husband and I had arrived in Avila during the week leading up to Easter. Local Spaniards were busy with Easter celebrations, parading large, colorful, plastic statues of Christ through the cobbled streets. We stayed a few days, exploring the sacred places associated with St. Theresa, before leaving to spend Easter in the house of a friend of ours, overlooking the Mediterranean.

As an adult, I did not belong to any established Christian religion. However, the spirit of Easter always touched my heart. This Easter Sunday arrived in a still, crisp light. As I lay in bed enjoying the quietness of our friend's house and the warm layer of blankets on top of me, I became aware of the familiar presence above my head. The sensation of pressure on my crown seemed to be stronger and more persistent than usual. I sat up cross-legged on the bed and began exploring this energy presence. Instantly my familiar sense of being a separate "I" dissolved into Divine Light and unconditional Love. There was no longer a separate Sukie experiencing a radiant presence pressing down on her crown. Instead, there was only One, Light of I Am expressing as all existence including the individual human being called Sukie.

Initially, the ecstatic shock of Light of I Am embodying in the Sukie human was so profound that tears dripped down my face onto my shoulders. All traces of a separate Sukie identity had dissolved. The bed, the walls, the blue patch of the Mediterranean through the window, the clear dawn light felt as much who I Am, Light of Being, as the unhurried beating of Sukie's physical heart. Now there was only Divine Presence, One and many faces of One, Light of I Am simultaneously transcendent and immanent. As Light of I Am, I was whole, infinite and eternal Oneness - Light, Love and Life of Being expressing as all existence, all experience.

This realization of our true Divine nature lasted without interruption for three days. Then, without warning, it lost its continuity; collapsing into longer and longer periods of separate consciousness. One Divine identity condensing more and more often into a separate "I" experience. Unconditional Love, heart of Being, increasingly veiled by experiences of separation and its inevitable corollary, emotional desire and suffering.

As my consciousness contracted back into the familiar experience of separation I recognized the three day Easter experience was not merely another invitation and inspiration to awake into our Divine nature but primarily an initiation into unfolding It. Three days that graced me not only with a transformative experience of our Divine nature but also with the spiritual strength to guide and support the unfolding of our true nature. For these three days of grace, of awakening as Light of I AM, were powerful enough to transform my consciousness sufficiently so that henceforth, as soon as I recognized my consciousness had collapsed into separation (and sometimes that took a while), it was able to reconnect to the unshakeable wellbeing of our Divine nature, even amidst intense physical and emotional pain.

About twenty years after this three day Easter awakening experience I was shown a simple way to access and unfold our Divine nature, Light of Being. A way that allows the subtler Light energies of the higher consciousness now flooding the Earth spontaneously to dissolve the denser consciousness of separation and suffering, and unfold our true nature, Light of Being. A way that, due to its simplicity, is not only compatible with our busy lives but also with the nature of our time.

The preparation for receiving this simple way of awakening and embodying our Divine nature occurred one morning, in 1999, in a motel bedroom in Mount Shasta,

California. As I sat in silence in front of the picture window framing the snowcapped peak of Mount Shasta, a shining, blue/gold energy presence appeared between my body and the generous picture window. This radiant energy presence seemed as tall as the two-story motel and simultaneously limitless in size. It introduced itself telepathically as the Mikael consciousness, that expression of Divine consciousness known in western traditions as Archangel Michael and by other names in other traditions. In the living language of Light, translated here into human language, Mikael explained:

"I am the one Light of Being that we are and simultaneously an emissary for this time of human awakening from the sleep of separation and suffering into Light of Being. I Am Light of Being and, simultaneously, a living voice and face of Light of Being. I am present at this Earth time to serve the awakening of humanity for I know the passages of transformation whereby Light of Being condenses as human mind, heart and body, and, therefore, the passages of transformation whereby personal mind, heart and body remember themselves as one Divine mind, heart and body, Light/Love/Life of Being.

"I have waited until this time to invite not only your minds and hearts, but also your bodies to align with and, thereby, metamorphose into Divine mind, heart and body since your human bodies need a certain level of refinement for the graceful embodying of Light of Being.

"If I seem to you to be something more elevated than you that is simply because, from the perspective of some, I am more awake to who we all are, one Divine Light of Being, Divine consciousness. There is, as you know, no separation, no otherness. Only Being

expressing at different levels of consciousness. In truth, you and I are eternally one.

"I Am here as a more awake expression of our Self, Light of Being, to assist humanity to awake as and embody Light of I Am. I Am announcing my presence now to those who are ripe to awake out of the long sleep of separation. I Am here to remind you that, while you are I, you have simply journeyed through a long night of forgetfulness. I am here to invite you to awake as and embody in your humanity the Divine River of Light/Love/Life that we are, for many of you are now ready to awake.

"I understand and honor that each of you relinquishes the experience of separation and awakes into the Truth of the one Being in your own unique way. I also know that, in as much as you invoke, allow, receive and embody Light of Being into mind, heart and biological body, your so-called personal mental, emotional and, ultimately, physical bodies, reflective of the experience of separation, will gradually and gracefully metamorphose, awakening as Divine mind, heart and Divine body/body of Light. From the ashes of the old human consciousness, crucified by conflict, greed, fear and service to personal self, you will awake as the one Light of Being. You will awake to the other as your Self, to Being All That Is. You will awake as the new human, the new humanity on a new Earth.

"Just as the energy of my presence, like a flame igniting a log into fire, spontaneously ignites personal mind and heart into the Divine mind and heart - Light/Love of Being, so too does the flame of Being, ultimately, ignite the cells of the biological body into Divine body of Light/Life. Since disease and death are simply reflections of the illusion of separation, they have no place when you wholly embody our Divine nature - Light of Being.

"Instead of leaving the body behind at death, humans will gradually learn, as part of your embodiment of Oneness, not only

mastery of mind and heart, but, ultimately mastery of body. You will unfold increasingly healthy bodies capable of dematerializing and materializing as needed. Bodies that, inasmuch as they embody Light of Being rather than the experience of separation, do not suffer the energy depletions, distortions and disease that reflect disconnection from the Life of Being that we are."

Soon after the Mount Shasta visit by Mikael, when I was back in my straw bale house high in the mountains of southern Colorado mountains, Mikael reappeared. While our first meeting was primarily an orientation and introduction to the Mikael consciousness, Mikael dedicated this second meeting to communicating the Mikael way of unfolding our true nature, Light of Being.

Mikael began by showing me the new Light now enveloping and permeating our Earth and solar system and explained that this subtler consciousness is the Divine blueprint of the new human and the new humanity. Mikael explained that this "higher" Light, by refining human consciousness, facilitates our ability to hear the knock of Divine Self on the door of our heart, to open the door and accept the invitation to relinquish the pain of separation, and embody our true nature, Light of I Am.

Mikael went on to say that this new Light enveloping the Earth is now sufficiently stable to begin unfolding our new Divine humanity. All that was necessary is for increasing numbers of us humans to awake as this one Light of Being and to allow it to flow into our personal bodies and our greater body, the Earth. Mikael explained that as more and more of us unfold this one Light of Being, Divine consciousness, our unfolding, in turn, facilitates the unfolding of Earth's consciousness which, in turn, facilitates the unfolding of Divine consciousness in more and more humans, since the unfolding of Earth and human consciousness is a co-creative process.

Mikael then outlined a way to awake and embody our one Light of Being. She/he (the Mikael consciousness/being is androgynous) suggested we allow awareness to rest above the crown of our head and experience the luminous consciousness of Being in and as the silent spaciousness between thoughts, images, emotions and sensations. She/he suggested that, if the experience of Light of Being seems inaccessible, we visualize Divine Light flowing "down" into our crowns, and contemplate this image of Light until we can experience Light of Being directly, expressing behind and within our visualization of Light. Mikael went on to suggest that, as we experience Light of Being, we surrender our experience of being a separate "I" into Light of Being, and allow the Light, like the sun melting an ice cube, to dissolve separate consciousness, thereby unfolding our Divine nature, Light of I Am, Light of all that is.[5]

Mikael explained that Divine Light, provided it is not resisted by the will of separate ego, flows spontaneously as River of Light into our crown, down our spine, into each of our energy centers (our chakras), and on down into our greater body, the Earth, itself a condensation of Divine Light, spontaneously dissolving the energy signatures of separation. He/she explained that as Light of Being flows into our heart center, our heart spontaneously experiences Light as Divine,

---

[5] Mikael, as a face of Divine Presence, Light of Being, is, of course, beyond gender, including both the masculine and feminine energies. Hence my use of she/he to refer to this spiritual guide, this Mikaelic level of consciousness.

unconditional Love, thereby metamorphosing into the one Divine Heart of Being. Similarly, as Light of Being flows down from our heart into the base of our spine, our root, our body spontaneously experiences Light/Love as immortal Life of Being, and, in time, metamorphoses into Divine body/immortal Body of Light.[6]

As we unfold and embody our Divine nature we gradually begin to live our Divine nature. Instead of relating, working, playing and creating from separate ego-consciousness, we increasingly relate, work, play and create as Light of I Am expressing as a unique human being living a unique life on our greater body, the Earth.

Mikael concluded by saying that while initially, we may consider River of Light as simply a spiritual practice to facilitate unfolding our Divine nature, Light/Love/Life of Being, in time we realize we are this "practice." We realize River of Light/Love/Life is our essential nature. Now, instead of practicing River of Light, we are awakening as and embodying River of Light/Love/Life.

During the many thousands of years since most of us forgot our true nature, there have been a few exceptional ones among us who either never forgot or who, in their Earth life, awoke from the sleep of separation and suffering. By way of meditation, prayer, ceremony, chanting and shamanic practices, these way-showers, often in high mountains, remote jungles and desert caves, devoted their lives to

---

[6] In some previous writings, I refer to River of Light as a light shower. I now call this inflow of Divine Presence the River of Light as this more accurately reflects the organic nature of who we are, one Being embodying Divine Light/Love and Life in our individual human experience.

unfolding and embodying our original nature, Light/Love/Life of Being. The radiance and wisdom of these exceptional ones kept alive the knowledge and experience of who we are amidst the long night of human consciousness. Often amidst rejection, persecution and, sometimes, torture, they allowed the flame of Divine Presence to unfold in their hearts and, thereby, shine into the heart of humanity, heart of Earth and all existence. These human ancestors of ours passed down the Light of Truth from generation to generation in preparation for our current time of collective awakening - the unfolding of the new human and the new humanity.

Hale Makua, a Hawaiian Kahuna was one of the more recent ones of these who kept alight the flame of truth. He taught that each of us are born as clear Light and this clear Light is a gift from our 'Aumakua', our immortal spiritual soul. Each of us, he explained, arrives in this world from the great beyond with our bowl of Light. This Divine Light is the true nature of all form. It is the energy of who we are, the intelligent energy of Source. As we move through life this Light nourishes and sustains us. However, Makua explained, stuff happens.

"Sometimes we lie. Sometimes we steal. And sometimes we injure others through our thoughts, our actions, or our words. When we step into the negative polarity, it is as though we put a stone in our bowl, and some of our light goes out. Slowly through time, our bowl of light fills up with stones, and our light dims until it is nearly gone.

"....The great problem in the world today is that the whole show is being run by individuals whose bowls of light are filled with stones. With few exceptions, there is no light shining forth from

their bowls, despite what they may think and proclaim, and we can observe the truth by their actions.

"....Hopefully we wake up to what is going on and discover what we are doing."[7]

When we do wake up and discover what we are doing, Makua taught, we can simply lift up our bowl, turn it over, and dump out the stones obscuring our true immortal nature - Light.

When we forget our Divine nature by allowing consciousness to contract by identifying with thoughts, sensations, emotions, gender, personality, personal will etc., with anything other than the One that we are, Light of Being, we experience the pain of separation from our true nature, Divine wholeness. When we relinquish and surrender all contraction of consciousness, all identification with any experience of separation and relax into and as the infinite, eternal, spaciousness of who we are, Light of Being, there is no longer the experience of a separate "I" experiencing itself as separate from you, rock, tree and God. With no experience of separation, there is no longer the experience of limitation and lack. There is only the wholeness, fullness and infinite potential of Being expressing as all existence, as all experience.

Inherent in who we are, Light of Being is heart of Being, Divine, intelligent, unconditional Love. As distinct from emotional, romantic love, dependent as it always is on the experience of otherness, the original nature of our Divine heart, causeless Love, is complete in itself. As our heart

---

[7] *The Bowl of Light* Hank Wesselman *PH.D, Sounds True, 2011, p. 47-48*

awakens as unconditional Love we, therefore, cease to yearn for Love, for now we are awake as Love.

Inherent also in who we are, Light of Being, is immortal Life of Being. As we awake, we realize that, while the forms and expressions of Life of Being may change, Life itself is eternal, immortal and immutable. This is reflected in the Light of Being dream described at the beginning of this chapter. For when the male and female bodies dissolve first into two Light bodies, then into one seemingly individual body of Light, and finally into Divine Source, Light of Being, their Life does not change. While their forms transform, their immortal Life of Being is constant - One Life expressing as different levels of consciousness. One Life expressing as different experiences, as male and female bodies, as individual Light bodies, while simultaneously eternally and immutably Divine Life of Love, Life of Light, Life of Being.

I Am Life,
stately cypress by Tuscan grave,
plumeria scenting Hawaiian sand.
I Am monarch butterfly and soft pollen,
succulent mango and orange blossom.
I Am nubile body in tropical pool,
quiet mist watering purple heather,
wind rustling tall palm,
and machete splitting coconut in search of thick flesh.
I Am sweet passion
soaring to enliven.
Full breath flooding blood,
rejuvenating muscle and cell.
I Am Life of Light,
Life of lily, snake and child.

My bodies transform,
my essence remains,
transcendent Being,
immutable flower.

As our physical vitality, our Life, rises from our greater body, the Earth, up our spine into our heart center, this Life transforms into emotions or, as our heart awakens, into the warmth of unconditional Love. As Divine Love energy rises up the spine into our crown center, Love can transform into thoughts or, as our awareness awakens, into Divine consciousness, Light of Being. And the other way round: the Light of Divine consciousness may drop down into the heart and transform emotional body into Divine unconditional Love. Love energy may drop down into our pelvis and transform into biological Life. Like water heating into steam and steam heating until it spontaneously transforms into air, Light/Love/Life of Being that we are is simultaneously water, steam and air, each simply a different expression of Divine Being.

As we experience different expressions of Light of Being, different forms, perceptions and densities of Being, we may confuse diversity with the experience of separation. For example, we may perceive sunlight not only as different but separate from rain, and a plant not only as different but separate from the rock. However, as we awake into our original nature, Light of Being, we awake as one Being expressing as infinite diversity of Being. We awake as One and many faces of One, as sunlight, rain, plant and rock. We awake as ocean and simultaneously as each unique individual wave. We experience diversity but no separation.

31

As we surrender separate consciousness and begin embodying Light of Being in and through our individual human experience, we begin the third principal unfolding of human consciousness. As we saw in Passage 1, the first unfolding is our original incarnation as Light of Being into an individual human body on our greater body, the Earth. The second unfolding is our awakening out of the experience of separation into Oneness, Light of Being. The third unfolding is embodying Divine mind, heart and Life of Being in our individual humanity. The fourth unfolding allows sufficient embodiment of Light of Being that our mortal body spontaneously metamorphoses into Divine, immortal Body of Light. By way of these four unfoldings, we complete our journey of consciousness from separation and suffering into the limitless well- being, health and creativity of our original nature, Light/Love/Life of Being.

As we hear the invitation to embody the Divine that we are, to allow the third unfolding of human consciousness, we recognize that in our forgetting of who we are we not only abuse, pollute and exploit mother Earth, we abuse, pollute and exploit our mind, heart and biology in pursuit of relief from the experience of poverty, conflict, ignorance and dis- ease. We recognize how separate consciousness fosters the desperation and greed that mines and hoards the fruits of Earth without gratitude and consideration for her needs or the needs of the rest of humanity, animals, plants, rocks and oceans.

We recognize the arrogance and ignorance with which we relate to our animal relations, how we allow our experience of separation from animals to justify our cruelty to and exploitation of them. We recognize how we condone corralling animals into factory farms, forcing them to live lives of unspeakable suffering until, with the same unspeakable cruelty, we slaughter them to feed our own bodies with their corpses, redolent with the suffering that defines their lives and their deaths.

We recognize the consciousness of separation creates and perpetuates political and economic systems that endorse control by the few over the many, money over compassion and greed over Love. Economic systems that, reflective of the experience of separation, flourish by pitting us against each other, that manipulate, coerce and brainwash us into becoming pawns in a pervasive and immutable culture of acquisition, competition, conflict, scarcity and war. Political and economic systems that seek to numb us to our innate Divine sovereignty, integrity, conscience, creativity, wisdom, abundance and wholeness by institutionalizing and promoting fear rather than Love.

Moreover, we recognize that the toxic mental, emotional, biological, political, socio-economic and ecological experience created by the consciousness of separation can never be healed by the level of consciousness that created it.[8] For separate consciousness always mirrors itself as the experience of conflict, pain, suffering and fear. Only realization of our true nature, one Divine Being, can birth a world of harmony, compassion, caring, abundance, wisdom and health.

As we look at the world our consciousness of separation has created we may, at times, find it difficult to recognize the seeds of a new human consciousness, a new humanity,

---

[8] The idea that a problem cannot be resolved by the thinking that created it is often attributed to Einstein.

unfolding amidst the hatred, greed, fear, conflict and disease. Yet, when we listen and feel beneath the cruelty and pain, we recognize the seemingly proliferating darkness is neither new nor growing. It is the same darkness that, in different forms, has distorted, tortured and dominated humanity for eons, but is now, by virtue of the Light of unity consciousness, enveloping the Earth, becoming more visible.

We recognize that more and more of us humans, not just the exceptional few, are now acknowledging the need to relinquish the experience of separation and suffering, and awake to who we are, Light/Love/Life of Being. More and more of us hearing and accepting the invitation from Light of Being to awake and embody the one Light/Love/Life and thereby birth a new humanity on a new Earth.

PASSAGE 3

Awakening into Being

Since perception reflects consciousness, when our consciousness condenses into the experience of separation, we perceive our self as separate from other people, from plants, animals, planets and galaxies. We experience a universe of separate, independent things interacting with each other in seemingly empty space. We walk through the woods and experience ourselves as separate from the trees. We talk with a friend and experience ourselves as separate from our friend. We feed the dog and experience ourselves as a separate doer feeding a separate dog.

When we experience a world composed of separate identities relating to other separate identities, we are like a ray of starlight that, forgetting its star nature, looks across seemingly empty space and perceives another ray of starlight as separate from its self. Instead of realizing each ray of starlight is simply an emanation of the one Light of Being, we forget the whole star that we are, and identify, instead, with one of our emanations.

Moreover, sometimes we allow consciousness to condense even further into separation. We not only forget the whole star, Light of Being that we are, and identify with one of its emanations, we also forget that each ray of starlight emanates from a star. Instead, we experience our ray of light, our individuality, as an entirely separate entity, entirely independent not only from all other emanations from the star but also from the star itself.

As we begin to awake from the experience of separation into our true indivisible nature, Light of Being, we are awakening as the one undifferentiated Being and, simultaneously, as each unique expression of Being. We are awakening as the One and the many faces of One; as macrocosm and microcosm, as star and each ray of starlight. We are awakening as indivisible Divine Self, as the eternal peace and absolute wellbeing of Divine consciousness, and, simultaneously, as Divine consciousness, Light of Being, expressing as different levels of consciousness, experience and perception. We no longer experience ourselves as an isolated "I" experiencing itself as separate from dolphin, flower and human, but one Light of Being expressing as the uniqueness of dolphin, flower and individual human consciousness.

Instead of experiencing solidity and separation, we now experience people, plants, animals and things as both unique and inseparable energy patterns and expressions of our one Self, Light of Being. We are awakening now as immortality expressing as life and death, Oneness expressing as diversity and polarity, unconditional Love expressing as emotional love and fear, Light expressing as light and dark. We are Divine Presence. We are the eternal now. We are peace and bliss of Being. We are infinite Divine potential, everything and no thing. We are unchanging Divine Presence, Light of

Being, and simultaneously each ephemeral experience of Being.

Now, when we greet our friend, there is no separate "I" greeting our friend, There is simply the experience of greeting our friend as a unique expression of our Self; greeting our friend as our Self. When we make love with our lover, there is no longer the experience of a separate "I", making love to a separate lover, but simply the experience of making love with our beloved who is both a unique, individual human expression of our One Self and, simultaneously, our One Self. When an angry driver cuts in front of us on our way to work, there is now simply the experience of a unique, individual human expression of Divine Self experiencing anger cutting in front of another unique, individual human expression of our One Divine Self.

Awakening as Light/Love/Life of Being, we experience essential ease, not because our days are suddenly without difficulties or even intense challenges, but because when challenges arise we now experience them as clouds passing through the sky of awareness. Never darkening the radiance of the sky, never veiling, impacting or even touching our essential nature.

I generally use the word "awakening" rather than "awake" as most of us experience awakening out of the sleep of separation as a gradual and unfolding process, rather than a one- time event. While a few of us may awake out of separation into the absolute truth of who we are, one Being, and never again experience our consciousness condensing back into the experience of separation, for most of us our early awakening experiences tend to be fleeting glimpses of reality, rapidly veiled again by forgetfulness. We glimpse our true nature, Light of Being, surrender our personal "I" into Light of I Am, and then, in the next moment, the habit of separate consciousness pulls us back into the experience of separation. Sooner or later we recognize we have slipped back into a separate identity, and surrender again into our Divine nature.

There may be moments in our unfolding in which we experience our original Divine nature as the limitless ocean of wellbeing in the background of awareness, infusing and condensing into the drama of separate consciousness. Then a time arrives in which we experience our eternal nature, Light of Being, moving from the background of our awareness into the foreground, center, background and circumference. Gradually, by way of grace and relaxed vigilance, we begin to notice consciousness collapsing back into the drama of separation less often and for less long; and the experience of being the One, both ocean and individual wave, beginning to stabilize. As this happens, our experience of our One Divine nature deepens, unveils and unfolds. Instead of fleeting, blissful experiences of being home, we notice an organic unfolding of the nature of our Divine home that we are.

While there is only one Divine reality, one Divine home, there are as many different awakening experiences as there are awakening individuals. Moreover, since awakening, is not a destination but rather a continual unfolding of our Divine nature, there are many layers or levels of awakening. Some of us, awakening into our Divine nature as no-thing, experience It as "emptiness", and, therefore, refer to It as the void. Some awakening first as heart of Being, refer to our Divine nature as unconditional Love. Some awakening as immortal Life refer to our Divine nature as Divine Life, or, like the ancient Chinese, as the Dao. Some, like practitioners of the Dzogchen school of Tibetan Buddhism, awakening into Being as Divine luminous Presence, refer to our Divine nature as the clear, primordial Light. Others awakening into Being as the one Divine identity, refer to It as Light of I Am or Christ consciousness. While still others among us, discovering the One Being through scientific methods, refer to it as the quantum field.

While the word "awakening" could be used for the second, third and fourth unfolding of human consciousness - awakening into our original nature, Light of Being; awakening as Divine mind, heart and body; and awakening as Divine mind, heart and Body of Light, it feels clearer to use the word "embodying" rather than "awakening" for the third and fourth unfoldings of human consciousness. For "embodying" places the emphasis on the experience of living our awakening in our human life; living, being and expressing Divine mind, heart and body in our relating, playing, working and creating. Living as the one Divine Light of Being shining as an individual human Being rather than living from the experience of separation.

Regardless of the many different catalysts of awakening, our first awakening experience, dissolving the veil of separation we confused with reality, offers each of us a direct, indisputable experience of our essential Divine sameness and Oneness. For many of us this first awakening, regardless of how fleeting, indelibly transforms our consciousness and, thereby, the nature, direction, and dedication of our life.

Hitherto, experiencing our self as a separate "I", disconnected from everyone and everything, including Divine Self, Light of Being, we searched outside our experience of our individual self for liberation from the pain and suffering inherent in the experience of separation. We looked to other people, things, situations, even to a seemingly outside God, for our wellbeing. We projected our essential nature "outside" ourselves.

When, for example, our relationship with our lover failed to deliver us the experience of wellbeing we projected on to it, we suffered the pain of disconnection from the wellbeing that is our essential nature. When our lover left us for someone else we suffered the loss of our experience of love. When we lost our job we suffered a lack of meaning and purpose. For, veiled by separate consciousness, we suffered each time we were unable to experience outside of our self, in work, relationships, situations and things, the wellbeing and wholeness that is our Divine nature. We suffered each moment we slept to our essential nature. For the experience of separation from who we are, Light of Being, is synonymous with pain. Pain is always an expression of disconnection from our Divine wholeness. At every level of experience, mind, heart and biology, it hurts to be unconscious of who we are.

Even though we may continue to experience pain and discomfort, mental, emotional and biological, until the whole of us, mind, heart and biology, relinquishes the energy signatures of separate consciousness and re-members our Divine wholeness, the instant we disidentify from a separate identity and awake as Divine I Am, we cease to suffer the pain of disconnection from our true nature, from Divine wholeness.

Awakening as the one Divine Self, Light of Being, we realize that each unique expression of Being, including the experience of pain, is simultaneously always Being, just as the TV screen is always the TV screen, pristine and untouched regardless of whether it is expressing as a horror movie, comedy or enlightened discourse. Awakening as both the One and the many faces of the One, galaxy, human, animal, rock, fear, joy etc., we realize each unique face of Being, regardless of whether it sleeps or awakens to its true nature, is always the one Divine Being.[9]

Awakening into our original nature, Divine Presence, Light of Being, expressing as all existence, is simultaneously an experience of both Being and becoming. While the one Divine Being that we are is transcendent, eternal and unchanging, our experience of Divine Being unfolds as our awakening into and as our Divine nature, Light of Being, deepens and clarifies.

While Divine mind, heart and life are simply different experiences of our one seamless, indivisible, Divine nature, the sequence of unfolding Divine mind and heart may differ for each of us. For example, some of us begin awakening out of separation by unfolding Divine consciousness, Oneness, and only after this initial unfolding feel the invitation to unfold Divine heart. Others of us, guided by intuition, devotion or prompted by the relentless teacher of emotional pain, may first open to heart unfolding, and, only after the heart begins to unfold Divine intelligent, unconditional Love, feel the invitation to awake as Divine consciousness, Light of Being.

Moreover, our individual embodiment of our one Divine nature also unfolds by way of different psychological, physical and spiritual practices, different life experiences, cultural traditions and, sometimes, different lives. Each of us,

---

[9] I am grateful to Rupert Spira for the TV screen analogy.

in other words, unfolds our Divine nature, Light/Love of Being, in the way in which we are ready to unfold. There is neither one way nor one right or better way.

While unfolding Divine mind and heart does not happen in any particular order, the unfolding of Divine health depends on our experience of Divine consciousness, Light of I Am, and unconditional Love being sufficiently stable. When we energize thoughts, beliefs and emotions reflective of separation and, therefore, suffering, these thoughts, beliefs and emotions express biologically as the chemistry of mental, emotional dis-ease. In time, this chemistry of dis-ease expresses as biological degeneration and disease. Only when both mind and heart are continually unfolding our Divine nature, Light/Love/Life of Being, can we create the chemistry of health.

While, eons ago, collective western consciousness fell out of paradise, out of instinctual oneness into duality consciousness, and thereby embarked on eons of pain and suffering, infants still experience, if only briefly, instinctual unity consciousness.

This infant or pre-fall unity consciousness, however, is significantly different from awake unity consciousness. While, as infants, we may experience no separation between our own experience and that of others, no difference between our personal experience and that of our mother, the dog and the Earth, most of us, as infants, still sleep to our original Divine nature. We are not aware of being Divine consciousness, Light of I Am expressing as the experience of our infant body, our mother, the dog and the Earth,

At some moment in the first few years of life, at least for most of us, our infant consciousness of being instinctively one with all experience differentiates into the experience of separate consciousness in which I experience myself as separate from "you" and all existence. Separate ego consciousness can act as a transitional passage in the unfolding of human consciousness. It can be a bridge from instinctual, preconscious Oneness to conscious Oneness. A bridge that, by rupturing our pre-egoic instinctual Oneness and birthing the experience of being a personal "I", carries us into the suffering of separation that births a yearning for liberation from suffering through conscious realization of our Divine nature.

This bridge of separate consciousness, therefore, is no more than a liminal passage of consciousness, a journey in between the truth of instinctual Oneness and conscious Oneness. It is a bridge to walk over rather than one to avoid through nostalgia for instinctual oneness, or one to get stuck on through attachment to the habit of duality consciousness. The suffering, poverty, fear and conflict that underpin modern civilization are a direct result of billions of us humans hanging out on this liminal bridge between the worlds, instead of allowing this bridge to carry us through the death of separate consciousness into the paradise garden that is our true nature, and know this garden for the first time.

"We shall not cease from exploration
And the end of all our exploring
Will be to arrive where we started
And know the place for the first time.
Through the unknown, remembered gate

When the last of earth left to discover
Is that which was the beginning;
At the source of the longest river

The voice of the hidden waterfall
And the children in the apple-tree
Not known, because not looked for
But heard, half heard, in the stillness
Between two waves of the sea.
Quick now, here, now, always--
A condition of complete simplicity
(Costing not less than everything)
And all shall be well and
All manner of things shall be well
When the tongues of flame are in-folded
Into the crowned knot of fire
And the fire and the rose are one.[10]

The way of returning to our original nature, Light of Being, and knowing it for the first time, revealed to me by the Mikael consciousness, is shared here, as we mentioned, not because it is more appropriate than other ways of returning home, but simply because it is a way of awakening that resonates with our time. A way that helps us embody the subtler "Light" of unity consciousness currently enveloping our solar system, so that, like icebergs melting back into the ocean, our conscious and unconscious signatures of separation dissolve, and personal mind, heart and body, thereby, metamorphose into Divine mind, heart and body.

This way of unfolding and embodying our Divine nature is not a way that requires extensive hours of meditation or

---

[10] *Little Gidding V*, Four Quartets T.S. Eliot (1943)

monastic living, but, instead, a way that acknowledges and embraces life as our teacher, and includes practices within the context of life's responsibilities, creativity, relationships and play. It is a way that unfolds consciousness spontaneously as we awake as pure awareness, becoming aware of the silent spaciousness of Light of Being between our thoughts, images, emotions and sensations, and consciously allow Divine Presence to flow as Light, Love and Life through our mind, heart and body as we ground in our greater body, the Earth. It is a way facilitated by our heart's unconditional acceptance of all experience, mental, emotional and biological, as it is, and for as long as it is. A way facilitated by our gratitude for all that is, including life's most challenging lessons, and a way that, in time, spontaneously facilitates the surrender and dissolution of our separate identity into our Divine identity, Light of I Am.

Whether we realize it or not, Divine Presence exists as a spark, a seed of Divine possibility within each of us. Each of us has the potential to realize our true nature, Divine Presence. However, when eons ago our consciousness dimmed, veiled by darkness, many of us began to confuse the seed of Divine Presence with the experience of being a separate ego. Like an ocean wave experiencing itself as separate from the ocean, we began experiencing ourselves as separate from the one ocean of Being that we are. We forgot that

I Am One,
spirit of garden and garden of spirit:
wise and innocent,
desolate and free;

mortal and immortal:
body and lightbody.

I Am we who writhe in separation;
we who awake as peace of Being.
I Am tropical ocean and melting ice sheet;
frozen breast
and warm waters of heart.
I Am One who melts;
One into whom we melt.
One who embraces separation
until separation remembers itself as One.

I Am loneliness
and the love we seek;
known and unknown;
the lost and the yearning,
seeker and the found.

I Am us and our lover;
and the ache of desire.
monk and prostitute;
denial and embrace;
soaring passion
and the child we conceive.

I know, include and love the darkness,
and darkness does not know and love me.

I know and am the Light;
and Light knows itself as I Am.

I Am Earth raped by split hearts,
withered by forgetting.

I Am Earth awakening
unfolding her wings
to birth a fresh spring.

I am no thing.
I Am all things;
I know all things,
but not all things know me

yet.

As we awake as Light of Being, our emotional experiences
cannot veil or fragment our one Divine nature any more than
dark clouds can veil or fragment the sky. Our thoughts,
feelings, emotions and sensations cannot disturb our Divine
nature any more than the essential nature of a mirror can be
disturbed by a reflection within it. Since it is the nature of who
we are, absolute, Divine perfection of Being, to include all
experience while being disturbed by none.

As we begin awakening into who we are, Light of Being, as
our consciousness begins enlightening, our discernment and
intuition, among other attributes, are refined and enhanced.
We find it increasingly easy to distinguish between those
ideas reflective of separate consciousness and those reflective
of our essential Divine nature. While we acknowledge those
ideas reflective of separate consciousness as part of the one
Being that we are, we notice our consciousness elevated by
the living, transformative power of Divine truth. We
experience truth opening us to more of who we are and our

unfolding of the feeling/knowing sense of the truth of Being sensitizing us to more truth.

Spontaneously we notice ourselves knowing and understanding more. A friend, for example, might ask for our perspective on her work dilemma, and we hear ourselves spontaneously offering an insight that surprises us as much as our friend. We might experience a relationship issue in our life, and notice that simple awareness of the issue spontaneously unveils its resolution. We might notice a question arising about the nature of reality and experience the answer arriving like the proverbial light bulb lighting up. Increasingly we realize questions not only imply their answers but, as our consciousness enlightens, more answers spontaneously arise into awareness.

When the answer to a question does not immediately reveal itself, it may be that our ability to hear the answer is veiled by unhealed emotional wounds or by attachments to certain beliefs, concepts, attitudes or situations. Or it might be, for whatever reason, that this is not the right time for us to know the answer, for, sometimes our consciousness unfolds more as we embrace the discomfort triggered within us when we do not hear the answers that our emotional discomfort insists we need. Moreover, some answers cannot be found within the level of consciousness that asks the question. In these cases, gently and loyally embracing the question unfolds, in time, a more awake level of consciousness wherein lies the answer.

One way of refining our awakening, and, thereby, unfolding deeper truth, is to allow awareness to rest in the crown of the head and open into subtler levels of Light of Being above the crown energy center. Since Light of Being is absolute and complete Truth, there is always a level of consciousness that knows the answer to every question. So, we can, if it feels right, gently open to subtler levels of Light until our consciousness is clear enough to hear the answer. When, for whatever reason, the answer continues to elude us, we can allow our conscious and unconscious being to be cooked by the tension of unknowing, trusting the answer will arrive when the time is right.

When we experience an answer to a question or an answer to an unasked question, we are wise to discern whether the answer resonates with our heart and body; whether it feels true and appropriate to every nuance of our being. It is tempting for those of us educated to respect mental knowing over the knowing that arises when our awareness opens to Light of spirit or rests in heart and body, to ignore spirit, heart and body, and rely, instead, on the intellect for answers. While the intellect can reflect and translate Divine wisdom, it is also easily co-opted by the limited and ephemeral perspectives of our emotional desires, mental prejudices and unhealed psychological wounds.

While, as we have mentioned, the seed of Divine consciousness, absolute truth, lives within each of us, most of us, since the dawn of modern history, either forgot or neglected it. Conditioned by cultures reflecting the belief in separation - separation from each other, from the Earth and from all existence, most of us were unable to awake, unfold and embody our Divine nature. Fed emotions reflective of separate consciousness, like anger, hatred and fear, we grew up mirroring these emotions and, thereby, feeding our own anger, hatred and fear into the collective human cesspool of negative emotion. Reared by beliefs in separation and suffering, we energized these beliefs with our attention as well as by identification with our ephemeral personality. Like a seed in the desert, we slept to the truth of who we are amidst the inevitable chaos, conflict and pain created and perpetuated by our fundamental belief in the inevitability of separation and suffering.

Now that Earth is enveloped and suffused by a more awake Light, a "higher" level of consciousness, this Light is quickening the Divine spark of Truth within all, of us, not just the few. Regardless of whether we accept, deny or resist this quickening, whether we are conscious or unconscious of it, this quickening is underway. Like the sun melting an iceberg, this more awake Light is gradually and spontaneously stirring more and more of us from our long sleep of separation.[11]

As our mental, emotional and biological bodies are increasingly enlightened by this more awake level of Light, habitual thoughts, beliefs, emotions, sensations and biological tendencies, reflective of separate consciousness, spontaneously begin to dissolve and transform. Mind, heart and, ultimately, even biology gradually cease to reflect the consciousness of separation and suffering, and begin, instead, to reflect and express our original nature, Light of Being.

The River of Light/Love/Life practice offered to me by Mikael for the unfolding of our true Divine nature, and outlined at the end of this Passage, is both a daily meditation

---

[11] When I use the word "higher" I am referring to a more awake level of consciousness, a level of consciousness more aligned with our original nature, Divine consciousness. I am not making any value judgments.

as well as a momentary way of awakening or reawakening as Divine Self in the interstices of our days.

Like many spiritual practices, the River of Light practice facilitates our awakening as Light of Being, as infinite Divine Presence that includes each ephemeral emotion, thought, sensation and experience without our identifying with any; without collapsing unity consciousness into the experience of separate consciousness. Above all, however, River of Light is a practice that unfolds our divine nature, not only facilitating our awakening as Light of Being, Divine consciousness but also facilitating our embodying of Divine consciousness - our spontaneous ability to walk our knowing, to live our Divine wholeness in mind, heart and body in our individual human life.

The practice begins with resting awareness above our head, above our crown energy center, and opening to the peace, bliss and Light of Being, Divine Presence that both transcends, includes and is the silent, spaciousness between each thought, emotion, image and sensation. It invites us to allow our experience of being a separate identity to die into our Divine identity, Light of I Am, Light of Being expressing as each unique, ephemeral experience. It invites us to relax as the unchanging, creative potential of Being, the eternal Light that births all experience of limitation and change.

As we allow River of Light of Being to flow from above our crown into our crown energy center, and on down our spine into our heart center, our heart spontaneously, when we allow it, expresses River of Light as unconditional Love. Just as our crown center, flooded by Light of Being, spontaneously expresses Divine unconditional Love as Divine Light of Being. As our crown experiences Light of Being and our heart

51

experiences heart of Being, unconditional Love, the harmony of our head and heart unfold the coherence that birth wellbeing, serenity and wisdom.

As River of Light flows on from our heart center into our root energy center, at the base of the spine, the root center expresses Light/Love of Being as immortal Life of Being. As mind, heart and body allow, experience and shine the Divine river of Light that we are, our original, Divine human nature, Light/Love/Life of Being spontaneously unfolds.

Although the River of Light/Love/Life practice focuses on the crown, heart and root energy centers corresponding to mind, heart and biology, Light/Love/Life of Being expresses as a unique signature of Being, as well as a unique lens for Being to experience its Self, through each of our seven primary energy centers. Whole embodiment of our Divine nature unfolds as we allow each energy center to relinquish the energy signature of separate ego-consciousness and spontaneously radiate and express our Divine nature - Light/Love/Life of Being.

Energy distortions, reflective of the experience of separation, in any one of our energy centers veil the truth of who we are. When any one of these centers is distorted by unacknowledged and unhealed psychological wounds, we may, in moments, be able to glimpse our true nature, Light of Being but remain unable to live our true nature in daily life. In meditation we may experience the Divine that we are, but be unable to reflect and express this in our relating, creating, playing and loving; unable to allow our mind, heart and body to embody and, thereby, shine our Divine nature. Regular practice of River of Light allows our Divine nature, Light/Love/Life of Being, to shine into the distorted energies in our centers, healing them; transforming the energy signatures of separate consciousness into the energy signatures of Divine wholeness, thereby allowing our centers to radiate more of our true nature, Light/Love/Life of Being.

Although more and more of us are familiar with the location and nature of our seven primary energy centers, also known as chakras, I will briefly describe them here both for those who may appreciate a review, as well as for those who are unfamiliar with them.

The first center, as we have seen, is located at the base of the spine, within the area of the perineum, between the anus and the genitals. When we experience being present, fully embodied in our root center, unconditionally accepting any energetic disharmony in this center, we can feel supported and nourished by the Earth. We can also experience the opportunity to surrender our experience of being a separate life force, and awake as the one Divine immortal Life of Being expressing as all life everywhere, including as our individual, human body.

When we fully inhabit our second center, located in the lower abdomen, and accept unconditionally any energetic distortion in this area, we experience the creative energy of Divine Life. We experience our potential to allow energy to express in form, the ability, for example, to conceive a child, to compose a symphony, make love or build a cabinet. We experience the opportunity to awake as Self creating sense-perceptible experiences.

When we are present in our third center, located in the solar plexus, and unconditionally accept any energetic disharmony in this area, we experience the nature of Divine will. We experience the opportunity to surrender the personal will of separate ego-consciousness into the will of unity consciousness, and awake as Divine Will of Being.

When we are present in our fourth center, located in the center of the chest, and unconditionally accept any disharmony and pain in this area, we awake as the essential nature of the heart, as Divine, intelligent, unconditional Love. We experience the opportunity to allow the metamorphosis of emotional heart, reflective of separate consciousness, into Divine heart of Being expressing through and as our individual, human heart.

When we are present in our fifth center, located in the throat, and cleanse, unconditionally accept energy distortions within this center, we experience the creativity of the voice, its power to birth different levels of consciousness. The creative power of the tone of voice, for example, to birth the experience of peace or gentleness. We also experience the opportunity to allow personal voice, reflective of separate consciousness, to die into Divine voice of Being, and awake as sound/voice of Being.

When we are present in our sixth energy center, associated with the pineal gland, and unconditionally accept all energetic distortions within this center in the middle of our forehead, our capacity for subtle sight/hearing/knowing, our clairvoyance, clairaudience, telepathy and intuition, are gradually refined and enhanced. We also experience the opportunity to surrender the subtle sight/hearing/knowing reflective of and veiled by separate ego perspectives, and awake as Divine seeing/hearing/knowing.

As we are present in our seventh energy center, located at the crown of the head, and unconditionally accept any energy distortions in this center, we awake to Light of Being, Divine Presence in between, within and as our thoughts. We experience the opportunity to surrender our experience of separation, allowing the experience of separation to die into the experience of our true identity - Divine Light of I Am expressing as all experience, as all existence.

For some of us this surrender of personal "I" into our Divine nature, Light of I Am, unfolds by way of a transitional passage through witness consciousness, witnessing what is just the way it is. While liberated from much of the experience of being a separate ego identity with its package of emotional desires, resistances and attachments, witness consciousness may still experience vestiges of separation between itself and Divine Self, Light of Being. It may observe both the one ocean of Being and, simultaneously, the one ocean of Being expressing as each individual wave while, consciously or unconsciously, holding onto the experience of a degree of separation from that which it witnesses. However, the surrender of the final residues of separation unfolds for each of us, this ultimate death and rebirth awakes us from the virtual reality of separation into our original, indivisible nature, Divine Presence, Light of I Am.

As we awake as indivisible Divine Presence and, simultaneously as a unique, human expression of Being, as both ocean and wave, we are able to honor, unfold and appreciate our unique individuality while, simultaneously, experiencing it as indivisible from Light of I Am that we are, since, in relative consciousness, Oneness is different from sameness. Embodiment of our one, same, Divine nature does not necessarily create similar humans with similar destinies and life journeys. Even when we have accepted and embraced into consciousness most of the mental, emotional and biological signatures of separate consciousness, we may continue to experience, emphasize and express the realization of our Divine nature differently. While Buddha and Jesus, for example, both realized our Divine nature, they lived, shined and expressed our Divine nature in different ways appropriate to their different cultures, different individual missions and different times in the evolution of human consciousness. Each radiated Divine Presence in service to different passages in the unfolding of human consciousness. Buddha's life and teachings focus more on enlightenment, awakening into our original one Being, while Jesus's life and teaches focus more on embodying enlightenment; embodying Light of Being, Light of I AM as Divine mind, heart of unconditional Love and, ultimately, Divine body of Life/Light.

As we awake as Light of Being flowing as River of Light through and as our humanity, the meaning of the phrase "going with the flow" unveils a deeper meaning. We recognize that "pushing the river" not only describes the nature of life lived by separate consciousness, but the essential nature of separate ego consciousness. Since separate consciousness can only exist through resistance, through "pushing the river" of the Divine flow of Being that we are.

However, it is easy at moments in our journey for separate consciousness to confuse "going with the flow" with "taking the easy way out". It can be tempting to confuse "going the flow" with self-indulgence – numbing ourselves by way of drugs, sex or alcohol to avoid experiencing the pain of our unacknowledged emotional wounds. Equally, it can be tempting to confuse "going with the flow" with promoting our emotional desires and prejudices. Discerning the difference between our personal agendas and the will of Divine Self requires the willingness and courage to refine our ability to distinguish between the voice of Self and the clamor of the emotional desires and fears of separate consciousness.

As Light of Being, flowing as River of Light, we are infinite potential and possibility. We are one infinite, indivisible and indescribable, Divine Being and, simultaneously all "colors", all expressions of Being. Just as the sun expresses itself simultaneously as light, heat and life, so our true nature, Divine Being, is seamlessly Light of Divine consciousness, Divine, intelligent, unconditional Love and Divine, immortal Life. Each expression of Being, Light, Love and Life implying and, simultaneously, being the others.

As we awake as Light of Being, we may continue, at least for a while, to experience emotional and physical pain. However, we no longer, experience the suffering that arises when we identify with any painful experience; the emotional suffering that arises when, forgetting we are the clear sky of awareness through which the cloud passes, we collapse Divine consciousness into separate consciousness and experience our self as the cloud. Now, awake as Light of Being, pain is never all that we are. It is just one expression of who we are; an ephemeral storm, even an intense one, passing across the unchanging peace of Being that is Divine awareness.

Awake as Light of Being our experience of life transforms from an emotional and mental roller coaster, fraught with tension, desire, fear and conflict, into a dance of Being. Now, instead of being the drama, the virtual reality, enacted on the stage of life, we are the peace and serenity of Being expressing as infinite plays. We are the one Self that births, includes and accepts each play just the way it is.

We experience the spontaneity of life's unfolding. Doors close. Doors open. Life's situations simply unveiling more of who we are. Spontaneous doing and not doing. River of Light that we are experiencing and Being our Divine Self. Like a rosebud unfolding its flower, Divine unfolding of the new human Being and the new humanity.

Meditative Play: River of Light / Love / Life

Summary of Passage 3

While practicing River of Light/Love/Life of Being, can, like any spiritual practice, perpetuate the experience of being separate from Light/Love/Life of Being, separate from our essential nature, spiritual and psychological practices can also serve our awakening out of this virtual reality. The right ones and the right time can facilitate our unfolding until we no longer need them. They can help us surrender our experience of separation, unveil something of our original nature, heal our wounded hearts, and facilitate the embodiment of who we are in the play of human life.

So, I offer a guided meditation at the end of some Passages of this book for those of you for whom it feels useful. Each meditation is designed to facilitate experience and integration of the essence of the Passage it follows. Instead of offering these meditations as practices, I offer them as plays. Not only because "practice" suggests practicing to be something we are not, but because "practice" suggests discipline and hard work, whereas play suggests more of the nature of who we are - spontaneous, playful Being. The experience of playful, relaxed, focused presence, rather than practice, seems to prepare us better for the realization and embodiment of our Divine nature – Light/Love/Life of Being.

If it feels right, ask Divine Self and your spirit guides to facilitate your awakening and unfolding of who you are. For help is always available to us from more awake levels of consciousness when we ask. The One Being that we are spontaneously assists its myriad expressions, including our human expression.

Initially, as we begin the River of Light/Love/Life practice, with awareness resting above our crown center and opening up to the still, radiance of Being between, within and behind our thoughts, we may be aware of almost incessant mental chatter, punctuated by rare, brief experiences of silence and stillness. Once we notice this mental chatter along with our habitual tendencies to pay attention to and process these whirling thoughts, we can, instead, become aware of the silence behind, between and within them. As thoughts clamor for our attention, we can experience them simply as the energies they are, without collapsing consciousness into them, without identifying with them and without engaging with them. We can recognize thoughts are not my thoughts or your thoughts, but simply energetic thought forms traveling across the sky of awareness. By not identifying with these thoughts, emotionally reacting to them or mentally processing them, consciousness relaxes out of the contraction that is monkey mind into the radiant, spacious, serenity of its true nature, pure awareness, Light of Being.

Initially, we may experience Light of Being merely as empty space. However, as we open to and contemplate this seeming emptiness that is void of thought, image, sensation or emotion, the experience of emptiness refines and unfolds. Like our eyes getting accustomed to a dark space, we gradually awake to the empty space as living radiance, and, ultimately, as our one true nature, Light of Being - Divine Presence; the unchanging One expressing as all experience of change.

In time, different for each of us, our separate identity surrenders into Light of Being. We die as a separate, finite individual and awake as Divine Presence, Light of Being expressing as all that is, including our individual humanity. We awake as the One and the many expressions of the One - as the unshakeable peace and Light of Being.

1. Allow your awareness to rest above the crown of your head. Become aware of Light of Being, Divine Presence, between your thoughts. Notice the difference between thinking and being aware of thinking a thought. Experience the Light of awareness.

2. Notice any tension in your mind, heart and body that is resisting this silent, spaciousness of Being, and allow the tension to soften. Relax into the silent, radiant, spaciousness of Being.

3. Notice any separate identities you may be holding onto - gender, age, race, separate "I" etc. – and, if it feels right, surrender these experiences of separation, these separate identities into our true nature, Light of Being. Allow personal, separate "I" to die into the One Light of I Am. Allow Light of Being to melt into its Self all residual traces and experiences of a separate "I", like the sun melting an ice cube. Be no one, doing nothing, going nowhere.

4. Explore Light of Being that we are - the unchanging, pristine, perfection of Being that expresses as all change while never touched by change.

5. Allow, invoke, feel or, if necessary, visualize Light of Being flowing into your crown center, and experience

your crown center shining Light of Being - Divine Presence.

6. Now allow Light of Being to flow, as River of Light, from your crown center down your spine into your heart, and allow your heart to express Light of Being as Divine, intelligent, unconditional Love. If it feels helpful, place your hand on your heart to facilitate awareness of your heart center.

7. Open to the experience of the harmony between your crown and heart center – One Divine Being expressing as Light and Love.

8. Now, allow River of Light to flow down from your heart into your root center. If it feels useful, place your hand on your pelvis to facilitate awareness of your root center. Open to the experience your root center expressing River of Light/Love as immortal Life, Life of Being, Life of all that is.

9. Allow River of Light/Love/Life to flow down your spine into the heart of our greater body, the Earth, and allow the vitality of Earth to flow into your root center, and up your spine into all your energy centers, suffusing every cell of your body, heart and mind with vitality and health.

10. Experience the harmony and wholeness that is Divine mind/heart and body – Divine Light/Love/Life of Being – the new human.

The Mini version of River of Light Meditative Play

The mini version of the River of Light/Love/Life meditative play can be experienced in a minute or two frequently throughout your day. Each time we experience either the long or mini version of the River of Light/Love/Life play, our mind, heart and body are infused, permeated and enlightened by the patterns, energies and Presence of our original, Divine nature, and, thereby, to some degree, metamorphosed into their original, Divine nature.

1. Allow awareness to rest above the crown of your head, and, surrendering all experience of being a separate "I", relax deeply as the silent, spaciousness of Light of Being, Divine Presence, between your thoughts, images, emotions and sensations.

2. Allow your crown center to shine our Divine nature, Light of Being.

3. Experience River of Light of Being flowing from your crown down your spine into your heart.

4. Experience your heart spontaneously expressing River of Light as Divine, intelligent unconditional Love.

5. Experience River of Light/Love flowing from your heart, down your spine into your root center, and on down into the heart of our greater body, the Earth.

6. Experience your root center expressing River of Light/Love as Divine, immortal Life.

7. Experience the oneness and harmony of Divine Being of Light/Love/Life.

8. Rest as Light/Love/Life of Being - Divine mind, heart and body of the new human.

PASSAGE 4

Awakening as Language of Being

I Am Light that we are.
I will speak;
and we will hear.

We will hear and we will know.
If we listen as the one that cannot turn away.

We will hear,
and we will know the wisdom we already know.
We will hear the truth
of who we are before the darkness fell:
the truth of who we are as the darkness lifts.

I will speak and we will know.
I will speak;
and we will know our Self
as the one who hears and the one who speaks.

As language of Light I create light and dark
from limitless potential I Am.
Human words suggest and translate,

but cannot reveal I Am.
Only Light of Being speaks truth of Being.

Only the living language of Light, the wordless language of Being, can communicate the nature of Being, for only Light of Being can express Light of Being. Since our Divine nature is simultaneously everything and no thing, human words, which imply something is not something else, can merely hint at and translate who we are.

When an insight arrives spontaneously and nonverbally like a "light bulb turning on" we usually trust it. We experience a sudden burst of light accompanied by the experience of nonverbal knowing, and a moment later we experience the mind's translation of this knowledge into human language. Such spontaneous knowing, registered as a burst of supersensible light, is a direct experience of the language of our original nature, Divine Being; a direct experience of the timeless, transcendent, living, language of Light. While we may not consciously understand the Light communication before the mind translates it into linear words and sentences, the "light bulb" experience offers us a momentary glimpse into the identity of insight and light.

As we awake out of the experience of separation into our original nature, Light of Being, our experience of existence refines, transforms and unfolds. Instead of experiencing our sense-perceptible world, for example, as composed of solid, separate objects existing in empty space, we now experience both sense-perceptible things as well as the space between them as different expressions of our Divine nature, Light of Being. We experience tree, rock, computer and empty space as Light of Being expressing as simply different energy patterns and densities. Moreover, instead of experiencing a sense-perceptible world as all there is, we now experience the sense-perceptible world as just one level of existence, one level of consciousness, one experience of our one Divine nature, Light of Being. We awake as different levels of the one Divine consciousness that we are, only one of which is the experience of a world perceptible to our five senses.

In other words, we awake out of a single level of consciousness, the consciousness of separation and physical sense perception, into one absolute Divine consciousness expressing as a spectrum of consciousness. While we may continue to live harmoniously within the parameters of space/time, and physical sense perception, showing up in time for appointments, not bumping into people on the sidewalk, we simultaneously inhabit subtler levels of reality unbound by the experience of time and space and the perception of solidity. While at one moment we may reach for the phone to call a friend on the other side of the world, we may, at another moment, at another level of consciousness, communicate energetically and telepathically with this same friend, without the need for a phone. Simultaneously, we experience both our friend, our self as well as verbal and telepathic communication as different expressions of our one Divine Self, Light of Being.

Now, each time we speak or write a sentence we experience not just the linear, sense-perceptible language, composed of sounds, letters and words, but also the living energy/being of the sounds, letters and words - the original language of Being before its differentiation into multiple human languages. As our awareness sensitizes, we become increasingly aware of the one reality that we are, Light of

Being, downloading its living language of Light into the human mind which translates it into human words and sentences.

My personal journey with human and, subsequently, Light language began with a powerful resistance to words, both spoken and written. One warm spring day when I was about fourteen, I stridently articulated this resistance to the universe. Standing alone in a moist English meadow, I declared loudly to spirit, or whoever might be listening:

"There are two things I absolutely will not do in this lifetime, one is to write books, and the other is to speak in public."

Although, at that time, I was not aware of the unhealed wounds inherited from other lives fueling my resistance to writing and public speaking, I was painfully aware of the intense fear triggered by both activities. So my potent proclamation to spirit on that gentle spring day in that moist English meadow gifted my emotional body a deep sense of relief. I walked home enormously grateful to have created a way of circumventing my fear.

For the next decade or so my adolescent declaration seemed successful. I did not write any books, just university papers, and I did not undertake any formal public speaking. Then one day, in the early months of my doctoral research on the feminine principle in Chinese culture philosophy, I became aware of a large energy presence bearing down on my shoulders. I had no idea what it was, what it meant, or, indeed, how to release my shoulders from this unwelcome weight. It felt like a heavy burden I was carrying around against my will; an energy backpack thrust onto my shoulders by some unknown force. So I quickly shifted my awareness from it, assuming that whatever this weight was would go away. I was wrong. The energy backpack remained on my shoulders day after day, week after week. It was there when I went to sleep, and when I awoke. Some days its presence seemed less noticeable. Some days, I even forgot about it. But, as the months went by, its weight grew heavier and increasingly difficult to ignore.

One morning, walking through a deserted, cold stone hallway at the university, the proverbial light bulb lit up, unveiling the nature of this energy backpack. I realized, with shock, that this presence on my shoulders was a spiritual "book" already "written" in the language of spirit, the language of Light, and waiting for my consciousness to awake sufficiently to be able to birth it in human language. I realized it was sitting on my shoulders because, at a higher level of consciousness than I could currently access, I had not only written this "book: in the language of Light, but also accepted responsibility for birthing it as a human language book. While, in that moment of revelation, I had no idea why, at a more awake level of consciousness, I had accepted this responsibility, it was unmistakably clear that higher Self, the spiritual author of this spirit "book", had neither interest nor respect for my adolescent declaration to the universe. It was clear that this spirit "book", sitting on my shoulders, was not going anywhere; that it would continue to weigh me down until I fulfilled my responsibility to birth it into human language.

Neither then, in that cold university hallway, nor at any later time, did I seriously question the authenticity, wisdom and benevolence of the spiritual author of the spirit "book".

My heart knew it was authored by a level of Divine unity consciousness that could only serve the highest good. Somberly I realized that, despite my resistance to writing, I would not only never be free of this presence of my shoulders, but also never be able to live the life I came to Earth to live until I fulfilled my responsibility to birth this spirit "book" as a human book.

So I relinquished my doctoral thesis, recanted my defiant teenage proclamation, and wrote *Uniting Heaven and Earth: Androgyny and Chinese Thought* (published in the United Kingdom under the title, *The Spirit of the Valley*). The book explores our human consciousness journey from instinctive experiences of wholeness and unity consciousness, through the pain and suffering of separate consciousness, into our conscious awakening as Divine unity consciousness.

A year or so after the publication of the book I dreamt that

I am inside a library of spirit books "written" in the living language of the Light, the original language of Being. This spirit library appears to contain the books needed to facilitate human awakening, at this time, out of the experience of separation and suffering into our original nature, Divine Presence, one Light/Love/Life of Being.

As I stand in the large, domed living language of Light library, in awe of the power and radiance of these spirit books stacked on the shelves of the high library walls, my awareness is spontaneously drawn to one shelf about halfway up the right-hand wall. Unlike some of the other shelves that contain many volumes, this one shelf is relatively short, containing only a few books. As I look closer I realize, with surprise and confusion that all the Light "books" on this short shelf are "written" by me. I see that they are "written" in the living language of the Light by my Higher Self, a level of unity consciousness that I initially forgot when I incarnated into a human body. I also realize that unity consciousness that I Am "wrote" these books, knowing that, by way of the challenges of human experience, my human consciousness would awake sufficiently to who we are, Light of Being, to be able to translate this living Light wisdom in human language.

I notice the first "book" on the shelf is the one I have just completed, "Uniting Heaven and Earth", while the other Language of Light "books" were, at the time of the dream, still waiting to be birthed as human books. They sit on my shelf in the spirit library with my name on them, waiting for my consciousness to unfold enough to give them a sense-perceptible form.

From the limited perspective of separate ego-consciousness, the idea of a spirit "book" already "written" by a subtle level of consciousness and existing on a shelf in the Language of Light library, while its human author still sleeps to its existence, feels more like the stuff of fantasy than reality. Such an idea only confuses separate ego-consciousness, conditioned, as it is, by the limitations of space/time consciousness as well as belief in absolute individual free will.

As we awake, however, as the One that expresses as many different levels of consciousness existing simultaneously, including the experience of individual free will, the existence of a Light language "book", authored by a more awake level of who we are, while its human expression sleeps to its existence, becomes more comprehensible. Since now, just as we may intuit, sense or recognize a spirit being welcomed into Earthly existence by way of biological conception, so, too we may recognize spirit "books" existing as living Light truth

71

prior to their conception, gestation and birth by a human author as human language book.

The dream about the Light library constellated many questions around the nature of spirit "books" and the language of Light. With time some of these questions have spontaneously attracted their answers. Others are still waiting, including a question about the exact nature of the higher consciousness of Divine Self that "authors" these living language of the Light "books". Like many transformative questions, this is one of those that cannot, it seems, find its answer at the level of consciousness at which it is asked. It is one of those questions that grows us, depending for its answer on our awakening to a higher level of consciousness.

Over the years since the dream, it has become clear that, unlike some channeled work which requires the consciousness of the channel to step aside to make space for the more awake consciousness to speak through the channel's mind, heart and body, the birthing of these language of Light "books" into human language requires the consciousness of the human author to unfold until it is sufficiently aligned with the more awake consciousness of the language of Light "author". It also requires the consciousness of the human author to be awake, at least to some extent, as the subject matter of the book.

This alignment between human and spirit author can then guide the human writing process. For when the human author writes a sentence that is aligned with the consciousness of the Light book there is the experience of harmony, rightness, between the human words and the spirit "author". When a sentence is written out of alignment with the language of Light "book" there is an experience of disharmony between the spirit "author" and the human author. Instead of the consciousness of the spirit "author" and human author being seamlessly one, there is now an incongruity between Light language and human language, and, thereby, a collapse of truth into semi truth or untruth. When this experience arises all the human author can do is press the delete key, and wait for the necessary resonance of her/his consciousness and thereby her/his words with the language of Light.

Such energy barometers of truth, recognizable as an inner experience of harmony or disharmony, are available to us all in each moment, whether we are channeling, talking to friends, composing music, playing or birthing a book from the spirit library. Much of the time, however, we are either unaware of the existence of these truth and rightness barometers, or ignore them, allowing, instead, more awake truths to be overridden by habitual beliefs, concepts and emotional prejudice reflective of separate consciousness. Gradually, as we begin to awake into our one Divine nature, Light of Being, we become aware that, in each moment, our thoughts, images, feelings and actions, are either in or out of harmony with the One that we are; either seamlessly one with our original nature or perpetuating some degree of separation and, thereby, suffering.

The language of Light is the original language of creation. It is the Divine living language that transcends experience of separation between word and meaning, word and creation, and "I" and "you". It is the Divine language in which the "word" and meaning, "word" and the essential nature the "word" describes are indivisibly one. Therefore it is a language that cannot be described or defined by linear human languages. It is the creative seed language, the essence language veiled by our "fall" into separate consciousness and the linear, conceptual languages birthed by separate consciousness.

Modern human languages cannot communicate the whole truth of Being. For they are birthed from and, therefore, reflect the consciousness of separation. Their pronouns, nouns and verbs, as well as past and future tenses, reflect a consciousness that experiences a separate "I" doing something to a separate someone or something within the context of the experience of separation that we call time and space.

In modern human languages, words, therefore, are signs, pointers to living, creative Truth, rather than Truth itself. When we hear the word "tree" in the English language our mind hears the word as a sound or sees the word as a combination of letters pointing to that which we recognize as a tree. Instead of experiencing the word "tree" as not only the essence and form of tree but also the spirit of the tree, the spirit creating the sense-perceptible tree, we experience the word "tree" as merely a lifeless, uncreative name.

While we are unaware of the language of Light, the language of creation, experiencing ideas as lifeless concepts disconnected from who we are, we not only impoverish our perception, understanding and creativity but, fundamentally, our experience of our Divine living nature. For, when we experience a concept like "tree" as separate from our self, our intellect may understand it, but we sleep to the experience of the word "tree" as a living expression of our Divine Being, and therefore that which both is and simultaneously births "tree" into human experience.

When we rely on the experience of seemingly lifeless concepts to communicate the nature of our experience we perpetuate our experience of separation from our Divine nature. While we may conceptually grasp or intuit something of who we are, we miss the direct experience of our Divine, creative nature and its diverse expressions. We miss the experience of being awake as that which we are communicating about. We miss the knowing that we create with every word we think or speak. We are like someone who has never stepped into the ocean attempting to communicate the nature of the ocean.

The language of Light, the language of Being, is Divine consciousness, Divine word, creative Truth, essence and form, all seamlessly one. It is the creative language of Being that, simultaneously, is, communicates and unfolds Being into all existence and experience. It is the living Word spoken of at the beginning of the _Gospel of St. John_: 1:1-5

"In the beginning was the Word, and the Word was with God, and the Word was God. The same was in the beginning with God. All things were made by him, and without him was not anything made that was made. In him was life, and the life was the light of men. And the light shineth in the darkness, and the darkness comprehended it not."

While the mind can translate the Language of Light into human languages, the language of Light does not require concept, word or image for its existence. And the translation will always be just that, a translation into a language that can only point, hint at or suggest that which it translates.

In the language of Light, the word "Love", for example, does not merely signify, suggest or translate the energy of

Love. It is not a group of letters pointing to Love. Instead, the Light word "Love" is the absolute essence of unconditional Love itself. It is the Divine, creative spirit "word"; a living "word" that simultaneously communicates, expresses and creates Love. It is a word that cannot refer to Love since it both is Love and, simultaneously, unfolds Love into being.

As we awake as Light of Being we experience Being All That Is, and Being the infinite potential of Being birthing into experience that which is intended, invoked and spoken. No longer experiencing human words merely as signs, husks, pointers to direct experience of Being, we are awakening as Light of Being, speaking Being into different experiences by way of the language of Being expressing as human language.

Awakening into and as the Divine, living, creative nature of each word, we become increasingly vigilant and discerning around our use of language; increasingly awake to the responsibility inherent in all communication. Our experience of human language is becoming radically different. Now, instead of a cluster of letters and sounds pointing to a meaning, we experience each word as a living essence and creative force, condensing limitless potential of Being into a unique energy and experience. Now when we speak the word "compassion" there is not only the experience of compassion as who we are, but also the experience of speaking the word "compassion" birthing compassion into our experience from our undifferentiated Divine nature, Light of Being, just as the undifferentiated nature of the ocean births each unique wave of its self into being.

As we awake as the Language of Light, we gradually cease to need books or even spoken words to unveil the truth of who we are, Divine Presence. Instead, as some indigenous traditions have never forgotten, we can begin to access the Language of Light, the truth of Being, directly without the need for human language and, for as long as human language continues to feel useful, we can open to a new way of experiencing it that quickens within us a direct experience of the language of Light. Instead of merely recognizing the meaning of words and sentences, we can move through the experience of human words into experiencing the language of Light. In so doing, we awake more deeply into who we are, Divine Being that is simultaneously source, womb, creative intelligence, voice, sound and child of creation.

When we stand in a dark cave it can take a while for our eyes to begin to discern shapes and shades of color in place of undifferentiated darkness. The same is true for our awakening as the language of Light. When we allow awareness to open to the possibility of a language of Light hidden within and beyond human words, our perception gradually sensitizes to the presence and nature of our original language living, as a forgotten seed, in the heart of human language.

As we open to the experience of human language as a door into the living language of Light, we awake to ways in which we can allow this Divine living language of Light to facilitate our unfolding and embodying of the Truth of who we are, Light/Love/Life of Being. Ways of speaking, thinking and writing that, by expressing our true nature, help us not only realize but unfold and embody who we are rather than perpetuate the experience of who we are not.

Meditative Play: Awakening as Language of Being

If it feels right, ask Divine Self and your spirit guides to facilitate the awakening and unfolding of who you are.

1. Relax in a comfortable position.

2. With awareness resting just above the crown of your head, accept unconditionally any thoughts, images, emotions and sensations that arise, just as the sky allows each passing cloud without being disturbed or impacted by it.

3. Experience the spacious nature of Light of Being beneath, within, beyond and around each thought, image, emotion and sensation, and, surrendering the experience of being a separate "I", awake as Light of Being.

4. As Light of Being, Divine Presence, notice any non-verbal knowing that spontaneously arises.

5. Explore the nature and experience of this non-verbal knowing.

6. Now allow your mind to think the word "health" or "wellbeing".

7. Allow the mental word "health" or "wellbeing" to dissolve and open to experiencing the energy expressed by and alive both within and as the word "health" or "wellbeing". Notice the radiant vitality of this energy.

8. As Light of Being, without words, allow the creative nature of the living language of Light to "speak" your

new humanity into experience. In the wordless language of Light, "say" "I Am Divine Presence, Light/Love/Life of Being living on our greater body, the Earth.

PASSAGE 5

Heart of Being

"Love is not love
Which alters it when alteration finds,
Or bends with the remover to remove.
O no, it is an ever-fixed mark
That looks on tempests and is never shaken'
It is the star to every wand'ring bark,
Whose worth's unknown, although his height be taken"
William Shakespeare Sonnet 116

As we awake from our experience of separation from each other, Source and all existence, we complete the second of the four principal unfoldings of human awakening. As we saw, the first unfolding carries us, as spirit, into human form on our greater body, the Earth. The second unfolding liberates consciousness from the experience of separation from our one Divine nature, and, thereby, from suffering the pain of this separation. The third unfolding initiates the embodying of Divine consciousness. During this journey Light of Being descends into mind and heart, enlightening them so that gradually our experience of having a personal mind and heart, reflective of separate consciousness, dissolves. We awake as Divine mind and heart, expressing as a unique individual human.

Regardless of the unfolding of our Divine nature begins with unfolding our Divine heart of intelligent, unconditional Love or with awakening as Light of Being, Divine consciousness, or both together, the unfolding of our Divine nature, at least during our Earthly life, is a continual process, with different experiences of unfolding quickening each other and, thereby, deepening our understanding and experience of our Divine nature.

Most, if not all of us, in our journey of Divine unfolding, will need to encounter our psychological darkness, our shadow. Our shadow contains distorted patterns of thinking, feeling, relating, perceiving and believing, reflective of separate consciousness, that our conscious mind rejects, represses and denies. It also contains authentic expressions and qualities of our Divine nature that we have forgotten or resisted. It includes energies that our inner judge, itself one of our shadow qualities, judges, such as anger, coldness, greed, dishonesty, hatred and fear; and it includes our buried gold - benevolent qualities of the Divine that we are, like compassion, courage, creativity and power.

As we venture into the darkness and find the courage to recognize our discordant energies, behaviors and attitudes, we may be compelled to acknowledge that who we thought and believed our self to be is radically different from who we currently are. We begin to recognize the illusions, fantasies, denials and unconsciousness that buttressed our precarious images and experiences of our personal identity and sense of worth. We see, perhaps, how we relied on the approval of our friends, family and colleagues for a surrogate experience of

81

Self-worth; how we tailored our behaviors to collective values, energizing those qualities that seemed likely to win approval from others, rather than unveiling and expressing our true nature. We may see, in other words, the many ways in which our emotions, thoughts and beliefs encouraged us to sing the song others want us to sing rather than the song we were born to sing.

We realize how, consciously or unconsciously, identified with the experience of being a separate "I", we buried those qualities deemed unacceptable by our peers to avoid the experience of rejection. We recognize, perhaps, how growing up in a culture that encourages competition instead of sharing, we buried our generosity and caring. Growing up within a community that believed only in those things perceptible to our five senses, we ignored or buried our awareness of subtle energies.

As we open to our unconsciousness, exploring the darkest recesses of our personality, we begin to recognize the disharmonious patterns of thinking, believing, feeling and acting we accumulated to protect us from the pain of experiencing ourselves as separate from each other, from the Oneness of all existence. As we see ourselves more clearly, our precarious edifice of self-worth that we spent years, maybe decades erecting, begins to crumble. We are humbled.

We realize we can only awake to our authentic Self-worth when we are willing to acknowledge and experience the fundamental untruth, and therefore essential worthlessness, of separate "I" consciousness. We recognize that only when we relinquish our attachment to being valued by others, accept ourselves as we are and allow the experience of separate "I" to die into the silent radiance of Being, do we unfold our essential Divine, Self-worth; the worth that no one can give us, and no one can take away since it is inherent in who we are.

For many of us, unfolding our Divine Self-worth significantly diminishes our experiences of emotional pain since it allows us to relinquish myopic visions for a transcendent one. What once seemed large, agonizing, emotional wounds now appear, from a transcendent perspective, more like emotional molehills than mountains.

Whether inspired by transcendent vision or compelled by the intensity of emotional pain, or both, the realization that the root of all emotional pain - desire, attachment and fear, is the longing for the Love that none can give us or take away, initiates the unfolding of our true heart.

As we explore our emotional "heart", acknowledge and feel our painful yearnings, we recognize the destructive patterns of behavior our experience of being a separate "I", with a separate emotional "heart", adopted in its misguided search for Love. We recognize our addictions to sex, food, negative attitudes, alcohol, drugs and codependent relationships, among other things, were all fueled by the pain of separation, by our unconscious longing for who we are - Love.

Until we allow Light of Being to shine through our heart as Divine heart of intelligent, unconditional Love we are unable consciously to Be who we are, and, therefore, unable to live who we are - unable to experience, express and reflect our original nature in our creating, doing and relating. While in meditation we may be awake as Light of Being, and perhaps as unconditional Love, in daily life, we continue to experience and express separate consciousness. Only intermittently embodying who we are, we continue, much of the time, to relate to others as a separate "I", desperately searching outside of ourselves for the Love that we are.

Confusing desire for emotional "love" with Divine unconditional Love, we live from fear and hunger rather than wholeness. We compete rather than share. We are judgmental rather than accepting and allowing. We are cold, or at least cool, rather than warm and compassionate. Compelled by unhealed emotional wounds, we react rather than respond. We mentally figure out ways of finding Love rather than allowing our life to be a spontaneous unfolding of Love. Our experience of incompletion, disharmony and separation births mental, emotional and biological bodies characterized by conflict, hunger and dis-ease. Our yearning for Love prevents us from realizing and experiencing Love as who we are.

Many years ago, I received a dream that revealed the importance of unfolding unconditional Love for the mission of humanity. In the dream

I am with my partner, a man with whom I have an intimate relationship. We are in the temple of Love. My partner asks: "Why do we come to the Earth?" I respond spontaneously: "To awaken as Love". He then asks "What is the purpose of Love?"

As I feel and ponder the refreshing sincerity of his question, I experience a brilliant shaft of Light flowing from Divine Presence that we are into my crown center and on down my spine into my throat. I taste and feel this Divine Light flowing out from my mouth as a living flame of Light.

In the language of Light, the flame of Light answers my partner's question about the purpose of Love, and my mind translates these Light words into human language:

"The purpose of humanity awakening as Love is so that the great white dove can fly and seed a new world".

While I did not understand what was meant by the symbol of great white dove seeding a new world, I was awed by the numinous experience of the flame of Light flowing over the surface of my tongue and out of my mouth. My heart trusted both the messenger and the message.

As I lived with the dream, over ensuing months, moving deeper into the dream experience of the living language of Light, the great white dove revealed itself as a symbol of our original nature, Light of Being. It showed me that each of us humans is not only a microcosm of the one Divine macrocosm, of the great white dove but simultaneously a microcosm of the one being that is humanity, in the same way that each of our biological cells is a microcosm of the community of cells that constitute the macrocosm that is our physical body.

The dove also revealed that, since each of us contains not only the seed of the one Divine heart but also the seed of the one heart of humanity, unfolding our Divine heart allows us not only to awake as Divine heart of Being, but, simultaneously, to awake as Divine heart of the one being that is humanity, and, thereby, spontaneously, birth a new world of inclusiveness, caring and harmony. A new human culture in which each individual is not only awake as Divine Being, but simultaneously as a unique and inseparable expression of the one being that is humanity, itself a unique expression of Divine Being.

Moreover, the great white dove revealed that humanity was originally spiritually "seeded" with the spark of Divine consciousness and, thereby, the potential for conscious realization of our Divine nature, by a more evolved collective consciousness, expressing as a multitude of individual beings, from a different area of our galaxy. Since this collective consciousness, unlike our current collective human consciousness, was already consciously unfolding our Divine heart, it was able to seed humanity with the spark of Divine Light/Love/Life of Being, and, thereby, with the potential to unfold Divine consciousness.

The dove further revealed that it is not just individual humans who arrive on Earth with life missions, but that collective beings, like the being of humanity, also have missions. It revealed that when we humans, and, thereby, our one humanity, unfold and embody Divine consciousness, including Divine heart of unconditional Love, it will be our mission to "fly" to another world, to ascend in consciousness, in other words, and seed those living in that other world with the potential also to unfold their Divine nature. The dove explained that this seeding of others with the spark of Divine consciousness is true service, not service to others whom we experience as separate from our self, but service to others whom we know and experience as our Self.

Love is not only who we are, heart of Being, Love is also the precondition of our return to the paradise garden, the golden age before our fall into separate consciousness. Only when we surrender conditional love, the hallmark of the separate ego heart that disconnects us from ourselves, each other, the Earth and all existence, can we awake as Love. Only as Love are we awake as one Divine humanity expressing as billions of individual Divine human beings inhabiting our greater body, the Divine Earth, and, therefore, only as Love everything and everyone as our Self can we rebirth our paradise garden and, in the words of T.S. Eliot: "know it consciously for the first time."[12]

A few of the most fortunate of us grew up with parents and caregivers whose hearts were awake, at least sometimes, as Divine, unconditional Love. When these fortunate few heard their caregivers saying "I love you" they, consciously or unconsciously, experienced themselves being unconditionally loved just the way they were. However, for many of us, our introduction to love arrived by way of parents and caregivers for whom authentic Love was, to a lesser or greater extent, contaminated by emotional agendas and attachments. Since emotional agendas and attachment were often all their psychologically wounded parents, when they were children, received from their psychologically wounded parents.

When a psychologically wounded parent says to the child, "I love you", these words may mean something different from Love. "I love you" spoken by a mother's unhealed heart more often than not is conditional love. Conditional parental love loves the child as long as the parent perceives her child behaving in ways that the parent values. Unconditional Love loves the child continually, just the way she is, even while the child seems to be behaving inappropriately; even while the

---

[12] *Little Gidding V*, Four Quartets *T.S. Eliot (1943)*

parent is attempting to guide the child into more appropriate ways.

Growing up within the precarious web of emotional dependence and emotional bargains inherent in conditional love, we grow up experiencing that as soon as we cease to play our part in this co-dependent game of conditional "love" the energy of love rapidly transmutes into blame, criticism, coldness, judgment, jealousy or even hate.

Many of us, therefore, grow up with little or no experience of authentic Love, Love that needs no one and no thing in order to exist. Love that shines unconditionally and eternally on all that is. Emerging from childhood with little or no experience of Love as the unchanging nature of the heart, we venture into adolescence unaware that Love, unlike conditional "love", is who we are, heart of Being - unconditioned and unconditional.

As we begin dating, and, once again, hear and speak the words, "I love you", we experience these words, consciously or unconsciously, as synonymous with emotional hunger, attachment and co-dependence. We experience "I love you" as meaning I am feeling a wave of love because you are relating to me emotionally in a way that satisfies my emotional desires, or my heart is loving you as long as your heart is loving me. In other words, we experience a whole truckload of emotional desires, preferences and conditions wrapped up in a package labeled romantic "love".

Until our heart begins awakening, therefore, we tend to confuse possession, jealousy and emotional attachment with Love. We also tend to confuse romantically falling "in love", experiencing waves of Love arising within us in reaction to our experience of another, with Divine, intelligent, unconditional Love. In our illusory belief that Love is something we can only get from our interaction with others, rather than the heart of who we are, we create a world of emotional drama; a world of pain, conflict and fear. In our desperate hunger for Love, we may even abuse ourselves, our children, animals and nature. We may run ourselves ragged searching for who we already are. Even when we notice our own emotional hungers and wounds distorting and veiling our heart's ability to shine its true nature, unconditional Love, our unhealed psychological wounds may continue, at least for a while, to keep our heart hostage to conditional "love".

As long as we inhabit separate consciousness, experiencing separation from each other and Divine Self, and, therefore, looking to others for the experience of Love, we grow a personal, emotional "heart" reflective of forgetting our essential, Divine heart. While comfortable and uncomfortable emotions may feel very real, we forget that they have nothing to do with the true nature of the heart, and everything to do with what it is not.

Our emotional bodies are little more than bundles of energetic wounds and hungers, all expressions of our loss of wholeness, our fall into the experience of separation from heart of Being, from Divine, unconditional Love. They have nothing to do with the core nature of the heart. Nothing to do with Love.

Emotions, comfortable and uncomfortable, are volatile, quixotic and ephemeral reactions to our changing experience of life. Our emotional body, for example, experiences fear of abandonment by our partner, excitement about a new romantic relationship and grief at the loss of a loved one.

Emotions are reactions, while Love is a state of Being. Love is who we are, rather than an emotional experience.

The awakening heart does not react to another's anger with more anger, fueling emotional drama with more emotional drama. Instead, since Love is calm, wise and consistent, the awakening heart quietly and unchangingly shines compassion into both our own and another's pain. It spontaneously radiates the wholeness that we are to each person, animal, plant and rock. Like the sun, it shines equally, eternally and unconditionally on each passing cloud and storm, responding creatively, intelligently and according to the highest good for all. The awakening heart may experience feelings of acceptance, kindness and patience, attributes of Love, regardless of whether our partner shows up for us or our boss appreciates our work. Since Love shines its nature regardless of our experience.

When we deny, repress, mentally process or seek to transcend our emotional pain by way of spiritual practice, our pain imprints its discordant energy in our cells, leaving the heart unhealed and our biology polluted by toxic molecules of emotion. When, instead, we unconditionally accept each emotion, we open a doorway into Love. For, when we accept unconditionally emotional pain just the way it is, without identifying with it and thereby collapsing consciousness into nothing but the painful emotion, we journey through surface layers of pain, the anger, for example, that protects us from the pain of loss, until we reach the core human pain - separation from heart of Being.

As our heart begins awakening into its true nature, Divine intelligent, unconditional Love, we may still experience painful feelings. We may, for example, experience intense grief if our beloved dies or leaves us for someone else, grief for the loss of our beloved and grief for the loss of human intimacy. However, since our heart is awakening to its authentic nature, unconditional Love, we can now accept and embrace the grief. We do not react to it with anger or judgment, nor deny it. Our consciousness does not collapse into nothing but grief. We do not elevate awareness out of heart and physical body into transcendent fields of Light. We do not chant mantras to distract ourselves from the pain of grief. We do not mentally process the grief, attempting to figure it out and fix it. Nor do we identify with the grief, and release our emotional reactions to the pain into our bodies, the bodies of others and our greater body, the Earth. Instead of all these exhausting and, ultimately, counterproductive struggles to avoid feeling our grief, we simply are who we are - Light/Love of Being expressing as a human who is unconditionally accepting into the hearth of her heart gut-wrenching grief just the way it is.

In the stillness of the night
We cry for Love's touch
forgetting that another can never bring us home.
In the heat of our desire,
with the passion of our loins
we seek and fail to find the ultimate embrace.

We struggle to love our lover and our friend;
believing love demands a willingness to bargain;
forgetting love is who we are;
that all it asks
is that we embrace the scabs that shield the heart,
so love can shine
the essence of who we are when we cease to try.

Love is not difficult to find.
Scriptures may speak otherwise.
But they were born amidst the night,
when only few
remembered.

Forgetting Love is who we are,
we may worship and revere the flame.
We cannot be the fire.

Love knows not like and dislike,
fear and doubt,
or theatres of emotion.
It greets rose and rattlesnake,
lover and thief,
with warmth that changes not with change of face
nor withers in the night.

Love warms as simply
as the morning sun;
and lights as quietly as the evening star.

Love awakes at dawn to our lover;
embraces him as our Self.
Love walks our path,
Allowing him to walk his;
walks together as two and One.

Honors his choice to walk alone;
loves him as much when he walks with another
suffused by heart too whole for hate.

As we unpeel the layers of emotional pain veiling our heart, welcoming each into the hearth of our heart, we reach our core pain of separation from Divine heart and unveil the infinite void of the heart. Instead of "my" heart, there is now only the experience of emptiness. As awareness rests with, in and as this emptiness, it reveals itself as Love - one heart of Being. Now each time life triggers into consciousness residues of separate, emotional heart - desires, antipathies, attachments and emotional reactions - we can unconditionally accept them into the hearth of our true heart, heart of Being. Like a flame igniting a log into itself, we can allow the flame of Love to ignite our residual emotional experiences back into Love.

In place of a separate, emotional heart experiencing people, animals, plants, rocks and stars, as separate and other, there is now only the experience of heart as heart of all that is. There is no longer the experience of an outside and an inside. No longer the experience of a personal heart relating to another personal heart. Only one heart of Being - Love expressing as each unique human. Love expressing as all existence.

Many years ago I heard a spiritual teacher describe his own experience of personal emotional heart dying into Divine heart. He was driving down a freeway in California and stopped for gas. After filling his car he sat for a while behind the steering wheel noticing some strange sensations in his chest. As he observed these unfamiliar sensations, he became aware of his emotional heart dissolving. Within a few minutes, he felt he no longer had anything he could call a personal, emotional heart. The center of his chest now seemed to be nothing but an infinite void. As he explored this void, he noticed planets, stars and galaxies revealing themselves within the emptiness. With amazement and gratitude, he realized everything in existence lived within this void, and that this limitless void was his true heart - Divine heart of intelligent, unconditional Love, heart of all that is.

Each of us experiences the dying of separate, emotional heart into Divine heart in our unique way, colored by our unique package of personal history, culture, psychology and beliefs. While some of us experience the death of emotional heart as a sudden radical illumination, for most of us the surrender and death of emotional heart into Divine heart of Being, like the death of separate "I" into Light of I Am, feels gradual and incremental - an experience of two steps forward and one step back.

The stabilization of a subtler, more awake level of consciousness, like the realization of Divine heart, requires us gently to allow the dissolution of sleepier levels of consciousness - those conscious and unconscious habits, perspectives, thoughts, beliefs, attitudes and emotions that constitute and perpetuate the less awake consciousness. It also requires relaxed vigilance, because, during the early weeks after unfolding a more awake consciousness, the mental, emotional and biological habits of the sleepier consciousness tend to pull awareness back into the previous, sleepier consciousness. For, over time, each habitual level of consciousness and unconsciousness programs our mind, heart and body. Separate consciousness, creating recurrent experiences of emotional conflict, limitation, fear and hunger, programs an emotional body quick to react emotionally to any experience of emotional threat.

The early stages of heart unfolding can, therefore, feel messy and inconsistent. Sometimes, like sunlight dissipating the clouds, we experience radiant heart of Being dissipating the clouds of emotional heart. Other times we notice the clouds of emotional heart reforming as our consciousness collapses back into identification with an emotion. So stabilization of the consciousness of Divine heart requires the ability not only to recognize when we fall back into sleepier, emotional heart, but also the willingness to surrender this resurgence of separate consciousness into the peaceful spaciousness of heart of Being. We need compassion, even gentle humor towards ourselves for each fall back into separation, as well as a gentle embrace of each moment of life not only as moment to unfold more of who we are, but also as an opportunity to do so playfully rather than judgmentally.

Gradually, for most of us by way of much patience and many bumps in the road, we notice our relating, feeling, thinking, perceiving and creating arising less from emotional body and more from heart of Being. As our experience of Being Divine, intelligent, unconditional Love deepens and stabilizes, so, naturally, does our experience not only of loving another as she/he is but also of loving the other as our Self. Instead of desiring, yearning and searching for Love, or experiencing Love momentarily by way of the ephemeral "in love" experience, our heart now increasingly shines the Love that it is, regardless of life circumstances, regardless of who "loves" or doesn't "love" us. Regardless, even, of those who dislike, criticize or judge us.

No longer compelled by the pain of disconnection from who we are, our life gradually becomes a spontaneous, unique expression of Light/Love/Life of Being, guided by the unconditional Love and wisdom of our Divine heart. As our ability to hear the inner guidance of the heart develops and refines, we realize there is no longer a need to make decisions. No longer a need to mentally resolve problems or search for direction, for now, there is no separate "I" experiencing the need to figure out the next step. There is simply Light of Being spontaneously unfolding, realizing and expressing Its Self through each human life. While we may not always understand why a certain path, word or action feels right to our heart, we are not only able increasingly to discern the guidance of the heart but also to trust this discernment.

Sri Bhagavan, the founder of the Oneness University in India, used to tell the following story to illustrate the experience of Divine guidance of the heart. He described how, when riding the bus one morning, a beggar sat next to him. Sri Bhagavan said his heart instantly felt it was right to give the beggar some money, and so he did so. The next day Sri Bhagavan was on the same bus sitting next to different beggar. This day Sri Bhagavan said his heart instantly felt it was not right to give the beggar money, and so he did not.

Sri Bhagavan explained that on the first day he did not know why his heart felt it was right to give the beggar money any more than, on the second day, he knew why his heart felt it wasn't right to give the second beggar money. Sri Bhagavan said there was simply heart knowing and trusting of this knowing - trusting the heart's experience of rightness.

Some years ago, just before I was due to fly to Australia, my body developed intense gastrointestinal flu. Witnessing my exhausted, feverish body, my friends, family and even a holistic doctor friend suggested I would be seriously risking my long-term health if I went on the trip. Fear thoughts raced in tempting me to cancel. However, I did not, for my heart felt the Light of Being flowing through every cell of my body saying that the trip needed to happen since it was the highest good, and that, therefore, I was going. While this gentle and strong heart/body knowing made no logical sense, and certainly did nothing to deter the barrage of fear thoughts trying to hijack my attention, I felt I needed to honor the guidance of the heart.

While the trip was physically challenging, never a day passed during it without some experience confirming the rightness of the guidance of the heart. Within a couple of weeks of returning home, my body, transformed by so much that had occurred while I was away, unfolded more health and resilience than it had enjoyed for years.

During each passage of unfolding our Divine nature, humble discernment is critical. The residues of separate consciousness, hungry for the energy of our attention, are quick and eager to seduce us into believing a choice motivated solely by our psychological wound, is, instead, prompted by the guidance of the heart. For example, an unacknowledged hunger for adulation might convince us that Divine guidance is suggesting we make a video to share our spiritual knowledge and upload it onto YouTube. Whereas the true motivation for making the video is our emotional hunger for validation, our yearning for the Self-worth that can only be found in our Divine nature.

Similarly, we might feel our heart "guiding" us to leave our partner and pursue an attraction to someone else. Whereas, in truth, the decision to abandon our partner at this time for seemingly sweeter pastures is motivated by our fear of experiencing a painful emotional wound triggered by our current intimate relationship, certainly not by Divine guidance. At another passage of life, however, it might indeed be the guidance of Divine heart to leave our current partner and embark on a relationship with someone else.

So how do we discern whether our guidance is coming from Divine heart of Being or from our unhealed psychology? While there are no easy or absolute answers, we do have some guidelines. Divine guidance, for example, always "speaks" with the still voice of unconditional Love. While its guidance may trigger intense emotions, and may, at times, communicate urgency, the voice of the heart is always benevolent, harmonious and loving; always clean of emotional agenda and drama; always honoring of our experience of free will. It never rebukes, compels, judges or criticizes regardless of whether or not we heed its will.

Unlike ephemeral emotional compulsions, Divine guidance does not come and go. It remains constant for as long as its message is relevant. While, amidst the cacophony of our emotional and mental noise, we may feel deaf to the voice of the heart, as soon as our awareness drops beneath our drama into the discerning nature of the heart, we find the same guidance waiting for us. We can also pay attention to synchronicity. Since sometimes the guidance of Love communicates not only as quiet heart and body knowing but also as synchronous events and circumstances, like the proverbial book falling off the shelf open at the exact page that answers our question.

Heart of Being loves as it guides us and Loves when we disregard its guidance. Sometimes, when we ignore the guidance of the heart we may seem, at least initially, to get away with it. However, at some moment or other in our journey of unfolding, we may pay a high price. This high price is not a punishment from God, for the Divine that we are, as absolute benevolence, does not punish. The high price may simply be a natural consequence of ignoring the will and nature of Being, ignoring the highest good. Just as a river dries up if it tries to flow uphill our lives dry up, or worse, when we walk out of alignment with the way and will of who we are, Light of Being.

If one morning, for example, we feel a disquiet in our heart about taking the usual route to work, and, ignoring that guidance for fear of arriving late, we get into an accident, this is not spirit punishing us. It is simply a reflection of what happens when the will of separate ego-consciousness, driven by unhealed wounds, agendas and emotional attachments, presumes it knows better than the guidance of Higher Self.

Ignoring the guidance of the heart, whenever and however it arrives, is, therefore, an invitation for trouble. Sometimes serious trouble. I learned this truth the hard way. I share my dramatic, somewhat lengthy, cautionary tale here in case it helps any of you avoid my mistake of allowing personal agenda, including genuine caring for another, to supersede the guidance of the heart.

My tale began many years ago when I was enjoying a rare opportunity to spend a winter in Hawaii. I was relishing the warm, soft embrace of Hawaii. Grateful not to be shoveling snow around my remote mountain home in southern Colorado; and eating out of cans until the long dirt road down the mountain thawed sufficiently for me to get into town.

As spring approached and with it my scheduled return flight to Colorado, my heart, indeed my whole body, felt a growing reluctance to leave Hawaii. Initially, I dismissed this reluctance, glibly attributing it to my enjoyment of Aloha. It made sense, I argued to myself that I would feel reluctant to exchange paradise for the intense physical challenges of my remote mountain life.

So, I continued with my preparations to return to Colorado, dismissing the reluctance of my heart as emotional attachment. However, as the days passed and my departure date loomed closer, the feeling of reluctance strengthened into unmistakable disquiet. Not an emotional disquiet, but more of a steady, knowing/feeling that I needed to cancel my flight and stay in Hawaii.

However, a friend of mine who had been caretaking my straw bale mountain home, monitoring the overland water line to prevent it freezing in sub-zero temperatures and caring for my dog, Braveheart, needed to visit his dying mother. I did not want to put pressure on him to delay his departure by sharing my growing reservations about returning to Colorado. So, despite my disquiet, I continued my plans to leave Hawaii.

While I felt pressured by this guidance of the heart given my imminent flight back to Colorado, its calm, loving voice exerted no pressure on me, but, instead, gently honored my freedom to go or to stay. Its unmistakable message was present when I woke up each morning and present throughout the day - a still, quiet voice beneath the surface busyness of my life. Increasingly I felt its wisdom, its benevolence and its love. However, I did not know what I could do to honor its guidance without hurting my friend, his dying mother and my dog, at least not immediately.

So, I started to bargain with this voice of the heart. I tried to figure out a way of honoring my compassion and caring for my friend while also, at least to some extent, honoring my inner guidance. The bargain my mental body figured out was to return to Colorado as planned so my friend could visit his mother, make arrangements to fly my dog to Hawaii, put my house on the market, and, as soon as my friend returned from visiting his mother, fly back to Hawaii.

It soon became clear, however, that this mental bargain with my heart did nothing to diminish the quiet, insistence of its guidance. Instead of sharing my guidance with my friend, and honoring his right to make whatever decision Love guided him to make, I decided for him. I protected him with my silence. I trusted my ego conditioned values around kindness and consideration above the guidance of my heart. I allowed my personal will to supersede the will of Love.

Suffused with increasing disquiet, I showed up for my flight from Hawaii. The short interisland flight to Honolulu took off on time and landed smoothly. That was the end of anything going smoothly on that ominous journey back to Colorado. While the flight from Honolulu to San Francisco boarded on time, the plane then sat on the tarmac for seven hours during which time I noticed my body beginning to feel increasingly unwell. It rapidly became clear that I was headed for trouble if I continued my journey back to the mountains. However, even then, despite this escalating sense of foreboding, I did not even consider getting off the plane. I still could not find a place in me that felt right putting my needs above those of my friend and his dying mother.

Eventually, the plane left Honolulu for the mainland. When, late at night, I reached my overnight motel in San

Francisco, I discovered that both its heating and hot water system were down. With no heat or hot water, my tired and increasingly unwell body found it too cold to get more than snatches of sleep.

Still, I did not contemplate turning around and returning to Hawaii. Instead, early the next morning, exhausted and sick, I boarded the flight to Denver. By this time I had no doubt that my body was in danger. How much danger I was not sure, but undoubtedly serious danger.

By the time the plane flew over the Rocky Mountains, in preparation for the steep descent into Denver airport, I knew with absolute certainty I would die if I stayed in Colorado. However, I still did not turn around in Denver and take the next flight back to Hawaii. Instead, I continued my journey, by way of a small commuter flight, to Colorado Springs. The only new decision my mind made in its ongoing bargain with the guidance of the heart was to put my mountain home on the market the following day, ask my friend to take my dog with him to visit his mother and take the first available flight back to Hawaii.

Essentially what I was saying to the loving, guidance of my heart was "I hear you, and I will do what you suggest. However, I will do it in my time and in my way. Even though I hear Love telling me to go back to Hawaii immediately, I choose to put the interests of my friend, his mother, my dog and even my property above the guidance of Love." I soon learned that bargaining in this way with Love is not a recipe for wellbeing.

The small commuter plane from Denver landed in Colorado Springs in a blizzard. My friend was not there to meet me at the baggage claim as we had agreed. Since in those days neither of us had cellphones, I just sat on my suitcase in the cold airport waiting for him. I sat there for seven hours. Another day and night passed with mere snatches of sleep.

Finally, my friend arrived to find me huddled over my suitcase, exhausted, sick and now very cold. He explained he had been unable to drive over the mountains in the blizzard. We arrived back at my house late at night to find that the central heating furnace was broken. So now I experienced a third night with little sleep, as I had to get up every few hours to feed the small wood stove to prevent the water pipes freezing and bursting in the straw bale walls.

The following morning, after calling a local realtor, putting my property on the market, and packing a few essential items for my return trip to Hawaii, I lay down to rest.

I awoke with a fever of 104F. It stayed that way for twelve days. On the morning of the twelfth day, while my friend was replenishing our food supplies in town, I crawled to the kitchen to get myself some water and felt a sudden, searing pain in my pelvis. After a few moments of resistance, I called an ambulance that took me to the local hospital where I underwent exploratory surgery.

When I awoke from the surgery, heavily sedated on morphine, and with tubes going in and out of what seemed like every orifice, the surgeon told me my colon had perforated. A few days later he said he had no explanation for the perforation since the lab had detected no evidence of disease. He warned my daughter I only had a 50% chance of survival.

After three weeks in the ICU, more surgical procedures and a battalion of intravenous antibiotics, my heart spoke to me again. It said I would die if I stayed in the hospital. My doctors told me I would probably die if I left the hospital.

However, now, finally, I had learned my lesson. I honored the guidance of my heart over the warnings and expertise of the well-intentioned, dedicated doctors. I discharged myself from the hospital. My loving and deeply concerned daughter took me home to my house in the mountains, where she nursed me back to a semblance of health. At least enough health for us to fly back to Hawaii together.

In this traumatic way, I finally learned that Divine Love alone knows the highest good, and it is, therefore, arrogant to allow personal will to usurp Divine will. Foolish and sometimes extremely dangerous to second guess or bargain with the guidance of the heart – unconditional Love, even when our bargains are motivated by genuine compassion, consideration and caring for others. I was reminded that only culturally conditioned "love" expresses itself in the same way in every situation. Whereas, Divine Love recognizes that every person and every situation is unique, and guides each moment of life according to the highest good for each of us, which, since there is only one of us, is simultaneously the highest good for all.

As River of Light/Love/Life permeates our mind, heart and body, our capacity to discern the guidance of the heart unfolds and refines. Confronted with life's crossroads, we notice an enhanced ability to discern which ways feel right, resonant with heart of Being. Even when the guidance of the heart conflicts with our residual emotional attachments, habits and personal agendas, we find ourselves increasingly able to recognize, trust and honor the guidance of the heart. Increasingly able to surrender personal will to Divine will, and entrust our life to Love.

Sometimes we experience the guidance of heart of Being arising into consciousness as an "ah ha" moment of unquestionable illumination and certainty. Sometimes guidance arrives quietly, gently and subtly, triggering significant emotional, physical and practical challenges. However our guidance arrives, we may wait a while, even years to understand it since some guidance can only be understood from higher levels of consciousness. Whether we understand the guidance of the heart or not, we trust it; acknowledging that understanding our guidance is secondary, both in time and importance, to hearing and following it.

From the perspective of the judgments of separate consciousness, the guidance of the heart may, at times, seem selfish and irresponsible. Since Divine Will may guide us in ways both incomprehensible and shocking to our personal values and conditioning. So plenty of practice and self-forgiveness are preconditions of unfolding our ability to discern the difference between our personal agendas and the guidance of the heart, the guidance of unconditional Love.

Integral to the surrender of personal agendas to Divine will is trust in Divine consciousness, and this is not something many of us unfold as we grow up in modern cultures. More often we are programmed from conception to believe that, once we venture into the adult world, we are on our own; that our very survival, physical and emotional, depends on us alone; that we alone have to figure it all out.

Unlike indigenous cultures, modern western cultures omit to tell us that our ancestors, guides, guardians and other more awake levels of consciousness are continually watching over us. Not only because they love us, but because they are part of us. Our parents rarely model for us trust in a benevolent, Divine universe that, because it is who we are, guides, protects, sustains and nurtures us. So we brave it alone. We struggle and effort rather than surrender, trust and allow Divine will to move mind, heart and body in whatever direction is the highest good for us and, therefore, all existence.

As we awake into Divine Self, Light/Love/Life of Being, trust gradually arises within the heart, and now our opportunity is simply to notice each moment trust disappears. To recognize each time doubt, fear and distrust, hallmarks of separate consciousness, hijack our consciousness once again, collapsing it back into separation.

As heart of wholeness, wisdom, harmony and Love, our Divine heart guides us to unfold our unique, individual expression of Divine Self, to live whom we came to this Earth to live; and to Love unconditionally, regardless of the changing weather patterns of life.

While the heart of separate consciousness experiences more than seven billion humans in conflict with each other, Divine heart experiences only one Being expressing as one humanity, itself expressing as seven billion individuals. It recognizes that all seven billion of us, as the Hawaiians say, are "in the same canoe". As we awake to being in the same canoe, the conflicts, greed, poverty and fear, reflective of separate consciousness, spontaneously transmute into respect, harmony, caring, co-creation and abundance.

Meditative Play: Heart of Being

Summary of Passage 5

There is only one heart of Being. This one Divine heart shines as heart of all existence, as heart of the being that is humanity as well as heart of each individual human being. When we experience a personal heart separate from heart of Being and, therefore, separate from all existence, including all humans, we yearn for Love. We yearn for Love from our friends and lovers. We yearn for what we already are, Divine, unconditional Love, and our yearning births our fear and pain. Our collective pain and fear births socio/economic and political systems reflective of this same consciousness of lack. As each of us individuals awakens as heart of Being, the being of humanity awakes as heart of Being, Divine, intelligent, unconditional Love, and this new humanity births socio/economic and political systems reflective of harmony, caring, compassion, abundance and Love.

If it feels appropriate, ask Divine Self and your spirit guides to enhance, facilitate, unfold and illuminate your experience in this meditation on the heart.

Experiencing the heart

1. Notice where your awareness is located in your body in this moment. Is it located in your head, your heart or your belly?

2. Place the palm of your hand on the center of your chest and breathe deeply into the area of your chest beneath the palm of your hand.

3. Notice any sensations, feelings or emotions that are in your heart and chest, and experience them fully, just the way they are.

Experiencing heart of Being

1. Allow your awareness to rest above the crown of your head.

2. Allow awareness of Light of Being, Divine consciousness, in between the thoughts, emotions and sensations.

3. Surrender the experience of separation, of being a separate "I" into the one Light of Being, Divine consciousness. Say to yourself, "Not "I", but Light of I Am".

4. Allow Light of Being that we are to flow down the spine into your heart energy center.

5. Allow your heart to express Light of Being as unconditional Love, heart of all that is.

PASSAGE 6

Unfolding Heart of Being

love is a place
& through this place of
love move
(with brightness of peace)
all places
yes is a world
& in this world of
yes live
(skillfully curled)
all worlds

e.e. cummings

I f we are to live who we are, it is not enough, as we have suggested, to awake as Divine consciousness, our heart also needs to awake. For, until our heart awakes as heart of Being, our life, including relationships, work and play, more often reflect the experience of separation and suffering than unconditional Love. Only when we cease searching for love outside of ourselves can our heart unfold its true nature. Only then may we Be Love - experiencing, embodying and expressing Love in all that we do, regardless of whether our days feel assailed by storms or graced by ineffable peace.

While many of us humans are conditioned to believe that our emotional heart, our emotional body, is the same as our true heart, the two are, as we have seen, essentially different. The chaotic energies of desire, aversion, fear, depression, grief, pride and emotional attachment that form, constitute and characterize our emotional body depend for their existence on the experience of separation from our true heart, heart of Being. Our emotional heart only exists while we forget our Divine heart.

As our Divine heart of intelligent, unconditional Love unfolds, we notice familiar emotions gradually dissolving, and unconditional feelings like joy, appreciation, gratitude, devotion and compassion, arising spontaneously. Now we not only understand but consciously experience that only disconnection from heart of Being, from Love, can plunge us into emotional reaction.

As River of Light/Love/Life, Divine consciousness transmutes all that it touches. It transforms the chaotic conglomeration of beliefs, judgments, opinions and concepts we call separate ego-mind into creative Divine mind, Light of Being. It ignites our baggage of psychological wounds, desires, likes, dislikes, fears and attachments, metamorphosing emotional body into Divine heart of intelligent, unconditional Love. Ultimately, it metamorphoses our physical bodies, including their cellular toxicity, degeneration and disease, reflective of separate consciousness, into Divine body of harmony, vitality and health.

The transformative flow of the River of Light/Love/Life "down" our spine into heart and body depends not only on our willingness to allow the "down" flow of this Divine River

110

but also to accept unconditionally into consciousness each thought, emotion and sensation reflective of separate consciousness.[13] When we resist our mental, emotional and biological energies, Light of Being is unable to transform and heal them into wholeness, since our Divine nature will not violate our experience of free will.

One of the ways we resist the inflow of our Divine nature, River of Light, is, as we have seen, by identifying with some partial experience of Self, like gender, race, age or even a passing thought or emotion. For example, when I experience that "I am irritated" or "I am female", my "I" separates its self from its true nature, the one Light of I Am, and identifies with a single emotional or gender expression of Being. In identifying with a part, my experience of "I" resists and disconnects from the whole. In disconnecting from the whole, I erect an energetic wall between my human experience and our Divine nature, and, thereby, obstruct the realization and embodiment of River of Light.

As we awake as Light of Being we continue to acknowledge and experience the infinite diversity of Being, including, for example, our gender and race. But we no longer identify with these or any expression of Being. We may enjoy our gender, but we do not limit our identity to it. Instead, we now experience gender as simply a wave of the ocean of Being, one expression of the Divine whole that we are.

Any time we identify with a part of who we are, we are energetically saying yes to that part and no to the rest of us.

---

[13] There is no absolute "down" and "up". It is only from the relative human perspective that we see River of Light flowing "down" and Earth energy flowing "up".

As e.e. cummings expresses in the poem quoted at the beginning of this Passage, our true nature is an absolute Yes.

As we awake as Light of Being, we may still, in our relative human experience, need to say "no" to someone. However, now we say "no" without experiencing our self as a separate human saying "no" to another separate human. Our "no" involves no contraction of consciousness, no experience of being separate from the other. While we are saying "no", we are awake, simultaneously, as the unconditional Yes that includes our own personality as well as all existence. For example, our heart might guide us to say "no" when our child asks us for something we feel would not serve her/him. However, while in the world of relative consciousness we are saying "no", our heart remains awake as the Yes that includes and embraces both the "no" and the "yes".

Identification with anything other than the one Being that we are, Light of I Am collapses unity into duality, and dualistic consciousness, perpetuating separation between individual and Source, inevitably prevents the unfolding of our essential nature – one Being.

As we relinquish resistance, however subtle, to the "down" flow of Divine Presence, River of Light, into our mental, emotional and physical bodies, some of our mental, emotional and biological energies, reflective of separate consciousness, spontaneously heal into Divine wholeness and health, without our awareness of this spontaneous, healing process. Like logs burning in the fire, these energy signatures of separate consciousness are spontaneously transmuted by the flame of Light back into Light of Being.

Yet some of our "stuff", different for each of us, seems to need our awareness for it to heal into wholeness. Sometimes this is because some of our stuff matures and elevates our consciousness as it arises into our awareness. For example, if we react judgmentally to our perception of another's anger and the River of Light spontaneously dissolves our judgment, we may miss the opportunity of becoming aware of the unhealed psychological wound at the root of our judgment of anger. We may be released of our tendency to judge anger, but continue to repress the psychological wound triggering our judgmental reaction to anger.

Until we recognize and accept this psychological wound, we not only continue to harbor its toxic energy within our mental, emotional and physical bodies, but this unhealed wound may continue to inhibit our ability to Love our friend unconditionally when she relies on anger to protect herself from her own unhealed wounds.

Each time we experience Love and any attribute of Love, like compassion, our ability to experience and express that Divine attribute of the heart strengthens. Since there is only one human heart, one heart of humanity, as any of us unfold an attribute of the heart, like, for example, compassion, the heart of humanity inevitably unfolds more compassion. As the heart of humanity unfolds more compassion it spontaneously facilitates each individual human heart to unfold more compassion.

When emotional wounds live unacknowledged and unaccepted by us, their disharmonious energy not only distorts our mind, heart and biology, preventing our embodiment of River of Light, Divine Presence, but their disharmony may also attract disharmonious life experiences.

Our unhealed anger wound, for example, may attract angry people into our life. Or, at least, encourage us to focus on the anger of another rather than on her/his other qualities. Our disconnection from our Divine Self-worth may attract financial challenges and/or colleagues who devalue us. Our unconscious pain and fear of being in a body may create physical exhaustion.

One of the primary qualities and expressions of Divine heart, heart of the new human is, as we mentioned, acceptance; honest, unwavering, non-judgmental, unconditional acceptance for all our experience, for our emotions, sensations, thoughts and perceptions. Acceptance of what is, for as long as it is, just the way it is. Such unconditional acceptance is not a thought or an action. Not something we think or do. It is a state of Being. It is who we are. When the sky accepts passing clouds, it is not doing something. It is neither passive nor active. It is simply being itself, being sky, and, thereby, allowing the clouds to be just the way they are, for as long as they are. The experience of passivity and activity only exists within duality consciousness. The heart of Divine unity consciousness is neither active nor passive but can express as either. It includes, allows and transcends all experience, comfortable and uncomfortable. Like the mirror that "accepts" each reflection just the way it is, without, itself, being touched by the reflection, Divine heart accepts all experience just the way it is, without its nature being touched by any experience.

For thousands of years, blinded by separate consciousness, many of us humans have considered it appropriate, even, healthy, to seek to minimize the pain inherent in the experience of separation. We have learned subtle and less subtle ways of resisting, avoiding, denying and transcending the experience of pain.

In pursuit of comfort and in flight from discomfort, we have become emotionally attached to those who like and approve of us, and emotionally resistant to those who dislike and disapprove of us. Like laboratory rats, our emotional bodies have become accustomed to gravitating towards emotional feel-good situations and away from feel-bad ones. Whether in flight from discomfort or magnetically drawn towards people and situations that feed our longing for love, appreciation and respect, our emotional body reflects and perpetuates the experience that our wellbeing lies outside our Self, in friends, colleagues, lovers, substances, status or an outside God.

As our heart begins to unfold its Divine nature, our consciousness may oscillate between separation and unconditional Love. A fleeting glimpse of Love vanishes as quickly as it arrived, shrouded again by our identification with a thought, emotion or sensation. One moment we are drowning in the inevitable suffering of separate consciousness. In the next, we are awakening into our true nature, heart of Being. One moment we are desperately searching outside of ourselves for who we are, and, in the next, joyfully awakening as Light/Love/Life of Being, grateful to have stepped off the emotional roller coaster of duality – happiness and unhappiness - into Love.

If we begin to feel trapped on an emotional roller coaster of pain, a dark night of the soul, it may not mean we have strayed down a cul de sac, but, instead, may indicate we are embarking on the next passage of our unfolding. Since, as we begin awakening into our true nature, Light of Being, like a light introduced into a dark cave, reveals our unacknowledged stuff, our psychological wounds, resistances, fears and desires which have lain hidden in unconsciousness, in some cases for eons.

When we identify with these surfacing wounds, our dark night of the soul can feel like a living hell. When, instead of identifying with our wounds, we unconditionally accept them into the hearth of the heart, the flame of loving acceptance transmutes our emotional wounds into Love. Our dark night of the soul passes. Sometimes forever, and sometimes to return a few more times, since our journey of awakening and embodying of Being can spiral round, and we can find ourselves experiencing familiar wounds from a different perspective or with a different level of consciousness.

As our capacity for unconditional acceptance unfolds, we not only find it easier to accept our friend just the way she is but also easier to accept the emotional pain triggered within us by our perception of our friend. Since our experience of unconditional acceptance is showing us that it is our own unhealed psychological wounds, rather than our friend's words or actions that cause our emotional pain; that our emotional pain has, in other words, little to do with our friend and everything to do with our unhealed, unwhole heart.

Instead of feeling the victim of another's unhealed stuff, we now appreciate the healing that unfolds as we recognize our unhealed psychological wounds reflected back to us by our perception of another, and, thereby, the increasing ability of our heart to respond rather than to emotionally react.

Awakening to the truth that we only suffer emotional pain when we forget the essential nature of our Divine heart, unconditional Love, we accept responsibility for our emotional pain and suffering. We also become more willing to venture into rather than resist our psychological wounds, since now we know that they depend for their healing on being accepted into the hearth of our heart wherein the flame of Love ignites them into Love.

While a few of us find it relatively easy to accept our emotional pain as it is, for as long as it is, many of us find unconditional acceptance undermined by entrenched mental and emotional habits of denial, judgment and repression. Habits of avoidance we adopted long before realizing our emotional pain depends on our unconditional acceptance for its healing. Well-rehearsed escape routes from the pain of our fundamental wound of disconnection from who we are. So, as we unfold the heart of unconditional acceptance, it helps to be alert to our default escapes from emotional pain. We may, for instance, rely on activities like watching a movie, going to the gym or taking on extra work as distractions. We may rely on blame and anger; blaming and berating another person, situation, or life itself for causing the pain. We may mentally process our pain; attempting to figure it out or seek to numb ourselves through addictions to food, entertainment, exercise, sex, drugs or alcohol.

Once we realize that life lived from avoidance of pain is an unending struggle to resist our essential nature, and begin, instead, to relax into unconditional acceptance, we may find ourselves struggling to relax. Our struggle perpetuates the tension that disconnects us from who we are. It perpetuates the illusion that in order to be who we are we have to effort to cease to be what we are not. It ensures the contradiction of shoring up separate ego-consciousness while, simultaneously, opening into the absolute peace and stillness of our Divine heart of unconditional Love.

As we relax into unconditional acceptance, we are able not only to accept grief but to do so without collapsing our consciousness into grief, becoming overwhelmed by grief, experiencing grief, in that moment, as all we are. Instead, resting as the heart of acceptance, we can gently allow the grief to be just the way it is. We can explore the emotions and sensations of the grief as we gently and unconditionally accept the grief into the hearth of our heart for its metamorphosis by Love into Love.

Unconditional acceptance, as an expression of Love, has, of course, no agenda. It shines from the heart of the mother who loves her daughter just the way she is, purely, freely and unconditionally, with no emotional attachment around her being like other children, doing well in school or developing certain abilities. As an attribute of Love, unconditional acceptance is like the sun. It does not shine on some people and not on others. It shines unconditionally on everyone and everything.

While the acceptance of the heart is always unconditional, unconditional acceptance does not mean we become victims of other people and situations. It does not make us passive. Unconditional acceptance, as an attribute of our Divine heart, is a state of Being, not a prescription for action or inaction. It is never a moral code of behavior. It does not dictate whether it is right to leave our husband or tolerate our boss's anger. It does not tell us when and where to draw the line. It certainly does not suggest we accept physical or energetic abuse.

Unconditional acceptance, as an attribute of Divine heart, simply accepts unconditionally what is, allowing Divine heart to discern right action and right direction.

As our heart softens into relaxed acceptance of what is, just the way it is, our experience of life transforms from conflict to harmony. Instead of lunch with a friend occurring amidst a cacophony of mental and emotional chaos, thoughts about the afternoon meeting, judgments about the food and emotional reactions to our friend, there is now simply the experience of our self, the food and our friend; and the experience of our self, the food and our friend is the experience of who we are, Divine Being expressing as self, food and friend.

Initially, as we venture into the heart of unconditional acceptance, we may believe we are accepting an uncomfortable emotion, whereas, in truth, we are stuck in our heads. We are thinking we are accepting rather than allowing the heart to experience and accept the uncomfortable emotion as it is. At times we may feel our heart is genuinely accepting the emotional discomfort, but then recognize our acceptance is conditional: we are accepting the discomfort on condition that acceptance dissolves the painful emotion within a certain acceptable time frame.

One way of unfolding the heart of acceptance is to allow awareness to drop down into the heart center, allow the inflow and outflow of breath to sensitize us to any emotions within the region of the heart and to feel the heart experiencing and accepting these energies, just the way they are. Sometimes it can be useful to invite into consciousness a person, animal or a natural scene that our heart finds easy to accept unconditionally and to explore the energy of unconditional acceptance before trying to accept a painful emotion.

One of my teachers of unconditional acceptance was my dog, Braveheart. When he and I lived in the high mountains of Colorado we were inseparable except for those times when he was racing down steep canyon walls to explore narrow valleys, inaccessible to my two-legged climbing ability. On cold winter nights, he lay next to me in front of the woodstove, and slept at the end of my thick comforter.

After a fresh snowfall, Braveheart's large black-haired presence would disappear exuberantly into the deep, powdery snow, and then leap into the air to gauge the terrain ahead, before disappearing again beneath the snow. When he was complete with his morning adventure, he would race into the house covered with muddy icicles hanging from his long fur. Often, before I could wipe his paws, he would leap onto my white meditation cushions, generously smearing them with muddy paw tracks.

While I did not relish the prospect of attempting to restore the white cushions to their zen-like purity, there was rarely a moment that my heart of acceptance closed towards Braveheart and his muddy paws. Although each time he tracked copious amounts of mud onto the white cushions, I vowed to become more vigilant about wiping his paws, my heart experienced only warm acceptance for him. This was more than I could say, at that time of my life, about some of my two-legged friends.

Most of us have experienced our version of Braveheart - a pet, a child, a sick friend, someone or something that, at least momentarily, quickens our heart into unconditional acceptance. Once we have felt genuine unconditional acceptance, we can deepen and stabilize the experience by returning to it regularly, until it is always accessible. On a congested freeway, we can allow awareness to drop into our heart and unconditionally accept the angry driver cutting in front of us. Waiting in line at the supermarket, we can unconditionally accept the checkout teller, exhausted at the end of a long shift. Like a young child learning to walk, falling, picking herself up and trying again, we can playfully unfold our heart of acceptance; compassionately and smilingly accepting our stumbles.

Accepting our emotional pain as it arises into consciousness from the depths of the unconscious can feel, at times, like walking into a fire pit. Seared by the fire of transformation, we may be keenly tempted to obey the voice of our conditioning that taught us to avoid fire pits; and, should we find ourselves in one, to leap out as soon as our feet register the hot coals. Even when we remain in the fire pit, unconditionally accepting the pain, its intensity may, at times, seem about to overwhelm our capacity for acceptance. With practice, we discover that nothing can overwhelm the heart of acceptance. Since nothing can extinguish that which is eternally so. Moreover, we discover that the more often we accept our psychological pain into the hearth of our heart, the stronger the hearth of our heart becomes; and, therefore, more able, more quickly to ignite our emotional pain back into Love.

Sometimes acceptance of our emotional pain into the hearth of the heart does not seem to result in healing. Our pain persists unabated. This can be due to a number of different factors, like the intensity of the wound, the consistency and authenticity of our unconditional acceptance, and the number of layers of unconscious pain underlying the conscious pain. Any residue of attachment to the dissolution of pain, any conditionality in our acceptance perpetuates the pain, for conditional acceptance is, of course, resistance to what is. When we resist fully experiencing and accepting pain into the hearth of the heart, we not only perpetuate an inner conflict, we also prevent Love igniting the pain into Love.

Ultimately, the art of acceptance carries our awareness down into our original psychological wound – the wound of separation from our original nature - heart of Being. This primary wound may first rise into consciousness as abandonment grief, triggered, for many of us, by the loss of an intimate relationship. As we accept the feelings of abandonment, the pain may diminish for a while, only to surface at a later moment, triggered by another painful relationship, for at the core of all abandonment feelings lies our original wound of separation from heart of Being. This primary wound can only find its ultimate healing when it is wholly accepted into the hearth of the heart, loved by the flame of Love into Love. Only then do we unveil that which can neither abandon nor be abandoned - us, our Divine heart of unconditional Love.

As we venture deeper into acceptance of what is, just the way it is, we relinquish the war between who we think we are and who we currently are, including our baggage of unhealed psychological wounds, yearnings, emotional attachments, judgments and fears. We not only resolve the war within but also the war between our-self and other. We accept our self as we are, we accept others as they are and we unfold acceptance of all existence as our Self.

122

Unconditional acceptance is only one attribute of Love - heart of Being. Devotion, gentleness, caring, compassion, gratitude and generosity are some others. Each is, simultaneously, an attribute of and a doorway into Divine heart. The attributes of the heart unfold spontaneously as the heart unfolds its original nature; and the unfolding of each attribute of the heart unfolds the original nature of the heart - Love.

Unconditional acceptance unfolds the quiet space in the heart that allows it to respond rather than react for now the heart lives the realization that our experience of another is never caused by the other but instead mirrors our conscious and unconscious thoughts, emotions, perceptions and beliefs. The following Sufi story succinctly describes this truth.

"A man entered the village and went to see the Sufi master, the wise old man of the village. The visitor said, "I'm deciding whether I should move here or not. I'm wondering what kind of neighborhood this is. Can you tell me about the people here?". The Sufi master said, "Tell me what kind of people lived where you came from." The visitor said, "Oh, they were highway robbers, cheats and liars." The old Sufi master said "You know, those are exactly the same kind of people who live here." The visitor left the village and never came back." Half an hour later, another man entered the village. He sought out the Sufi master and said, "I'm thinking of moving here. Can you tell me what kind of people live here?" Again the Sufi master said, "Tell me what kind of people lived where you came from." The visitor said, "Oh, they were the kindest, gentlest, most compassionate, loving people. I shall miss them terribly." The Sufi

master said, "Those are exactly the kinds of people who live here, too."[14]

In each moment our bodies are surrounded by immeasurable quantities of energy and information. We only consciously register minuscule amounts of this energy and information. So why do we register the energies we do? Why, for example, did we register the kindness of the bank teller this morning, and not the rest of her personality or, indeed, her subtle bodies? Was it just because her kindness was the most pronounced energy while she was receiving our checks? Or was it, at least in part, because of the mirror nature of consciousness; the nature of our consciousness, including unconsciousness, to resonate with and, thereby, be mirrored by our experience?

When we notice ourselves emotionally triggered by our perception of another's personality trait, we may be looking into the mirror and reacting to that same personality trait in ourselves. For example, when we react with aversion or judgment to our perception of another's arrogance, we may be reacting to our own unconscious arrogance. The arrogance that, perhaps earlier in life, we developed to compensate or protect us from feelings of inadequacy.

Similarly, when we are emotionally triggered by our perception of another's emotional coldness, our perception of coldness may mirror the coldness in our own heart; the coldness that, earlier in life, we adopted to protect us from our experience of rejection or judgment by our caregivers.

---

[14] *The Essential Spontaneous Fulfillment of Desire: The Essence of Harnessing the Infinite Power of Coincidence*, Deepak Chopra M.D. Harmony books 2007

As we acknowledge the mirror nature of consciousness, we open another door into healing the wounded, un-whole energies that veil our Divine heart. Instead of reacting to our perception of coldness in our friend with our own coldness, thereby compounding humanity's cesspool of toxic energy, we accept responsibility for our experience and allow our perception of our friend's coldness to show us where we rely on emotional coldness to protect us from unhealed emotional pain. As we accept this pain into the hearth of our heart, allowing the flame of Love to transform it back into Love, we are no longer triggered by our perception of coldness in our friend, Moreover, we may cease even to register the coldness in our friend, spontaneously attending, instead, on other qualities in her/him.

Since the mirror nature of consciousness applies as much to "benevolent" qualities as it does to "negative" ones, we can look into the mirror of consciousness to recognize our essential Divine qualities. When we perceive in others qualities that inspire and attract us, we can recognize these as attributes of our Divine heart that we are ready to unfold. For example, we can appreciate the compassion we admire in a spiritual teacher as the compassion our heart is ready to embody. Recognizing our readiness to unfold compassion, we can meditate on our experience of the spiritual teacher's compassion, feeling it and merging with it until our heart becomes it.

The process of awakening into consciousness and integrating hitherto sleeping attributes of the heart, like compassion, can feel like learning to sing a new song. At first, we hear the "song" of compassion. The tune is attractive but difficult to replicate. Our vocal cords feel awkward and unpracticed. However, as we listen more carefully, hear and feel the tune, practice singing it, our heart awakes as the song of compassion; and, awakening into compassion, it awakes into more of its Divine nature.

We can also integrate attributes of heart of Being by way of physical sensations. We can pay attention to the sensations in our chest when, for example, we are experiencing compassion. Then, when our heart feels disconnected from compassion, we can invite our physical chest to feel the sensations of compassion, thereby allowing the heart to remember its compassionate nature.

We can also unfold the attributes of the heart, like compassion, by way of acting, Feeling ourselves on the stage of life, we can invite ourselves to act compassionately towards another. In time the actor becomes the character. By acting compassionately we facilitate the unfolding of compassion.

A more subtle way of unfolding the attributes of the heart, like compassion, is by allowing the heart to feel and become the language of Light, the energy within and behind the spoken or thought word "compassion".

While unconditional acceptance of what is, including acceptance of the "mirror" of life, facilitates the awakening of the heart, the ultimate metamorphosis of personal emotional "heart" into Divine heart of unconditional Love is an act of grace. We facilitate this act of grace each time we allow Light of Being, River of Light/Love to "flow" through our heart, and surrender our emotional "heart" into the hearth of our heart for metamorphosis by the flame of Love into Love.

As personal "heart" begins to die, some of us, like the spiritual teacher at the California gas station, may first experience nothing but emptiness where personal "heart" once seemed to exist. Gone now is the noisy emotional body yearning for fulfillment. Gone are our likes and dislikes, judgments, attachments and fears. Gone is our emotional suffering. Then, in Divine timing that is unique for each of us, the void unveils its Self. Now, in place of emptiness, there is Divine heart of Being, heart of all that is. Divine intelligent, unconditional Love complete in itself. Love creating as all life everywhere. Love shining as our self, our lover and the Earth.

"In the fortified city of the imperishable, our body, there is a lotus and in this lotus a tiny space: what does it contain that one should desire to know it?"

"You must reply: "As vast as this space without is the tiny space within your heart: heaven and earth are found in it, fire and air, sun and moon, lightning and the constellations, whatever belongs to you here below and all that doesn't, all this is gathered in that tiny space within your heart."[15]

As we awake as heart of Being, Divine Love shining as each unique human life, and, simultaneously, as heart of humanity, we awake as Love's wisdom, intelligence, Presence, knowledge and creative power. Simultaneously, we awake into the humble recognition that our heart is a work in progress; humble recognition that all we can do is honor the wisdom of the heart as we feel it today, knowing that tomorrow may unveil more of the Divine intelligence of Love.

Without humble acknowledgment of our unfolding as a work in progress there is always, as we mentioned, the possibility of separate consciousness re-asserting itself and

---

[15] Chandogya *Upanishad* 8.1.2-3

usurping our unfolding into its service. For instance, we may have an experience of personal, emotional heart dissolving into heart of Being, and then a remnant of our unhealed psyche might rise up and claim this awakening experience as its own achievement. We might find ourselves feeling "I am enlightened" when there is no separate "I" to be enlightened. Only Divine Presence awakening, realizing, unfolding and experiencing its infinite potential by way of each, individual human experience.

As we cross the bridge of change, surrendering the experience of separation and unfolding our true nature, Light/Love of Being, it is essential to keep walking across the bridge. For only by continuing across the bridge of change can we can avoid the fate of Lot's wife (Genesis 19:25) who ignored the advice of the angels, looked back to the city of Sodom as it was being destroyed by God, and was turned into a pillar of salt.

As our heart stabilizes as Love, old emotional and mental habits, reflective of separate consciousness, gradually diminish and dissolve. The brain rewires itself. The union of Divine mind and heart, Light/Love of Being unfolds the new human. The experience of life as a prison yard or rigorous school room, reflective of separate consciousness, gradually transforms into the experience of life as a Divine playground.

Less and less is there the experience of a separate "I" practicing River of Light/Love/Life. Less and less a River of Light/Love/Life practice to be practiced. No subject and object. No agendas. No effort. No resistance. Simply Light of Being organically, naturally and spontaneously unfolding different experiences and expressions of Self. Seamless

Presence of Being shining, like the sun, simultaneously as light, warmth and life.

Meditative Play: Unfolding Heart of Being

Summary of Passage 6

Personal, emotional heart, reflective of separate consciousness, metamorphoses into our one Divine heart of Being by way of many different psycho/spiritual paths, but always by Divine grace. The path described in this passage is a simple process of accepting the energies of separation and suffering into the hearth of our heart, like gathering logs into the fire. As we allow Light of Being, as River of Light, to flow down the spine from our crown center into the heart, our heart center experiences and radiates Light of Being as Divine, unconditional Love. As we accept unconditionally all feelings and emotions, reflective of separation and suffering, into the hearth of the heart, the flame of Divine Love ignites the denser energies of our psychological wounds, emotional attachments, desires, aversions and fears into its Self. Separate, emotional heart, thereby, metamorphoses into Divine heart of Being – Love.

If it feels appropriate, invite Divine Self and your spirit guides to enhance, facilitate, unfold and illuminate your experience.

1. With awareness above the crown of your head, open to Light of Being, Divine Presence, in between thoughts, images, emotions and sensations.

2. Surrender personal I into Light of Being - not I, but Light of I Am, and awake as Light of Being expressing as all that is.

3. Allow Light of Being, Light of I Am, to flow into the crown of your head, refining and enlightening your brain and mind. Allowing your brain and mind to relax into alignment with the one Divine mind of Being.

4. Allow Light of I Am, as River of Light, to flow down your spine into the center of your chest, into your physical and energetic heart.

5. Allow your heart to experience and express Light of Being as Divine, unconditional Love.

6. Experience unconditional Love expressing as unconditional acceptance of your experience in this moment, just the way it is.

7. Accept unconditionally all your current feelings and emotions, including all emotional pain, into the hearth of your heart.

8. Allow the flame of Divine Love within the hearth of the heart to ignite all emotional pain into its Self - unconditional Love.

9. Allow Divine Love to dissolve your experience of having a personal, separate, emotional "heart" back

into Its Self- one heart of Being, Divine intelligent, unconditional Love.

10. Experience your heart as heart of Being - one Divine heart of all that is.

11. As Divine heart of Being, see and feel yourself relating to your friend, driving the car and walking in nature.

12. Experience Being the unity of Divine mind and heart, the unity of Light and Love expressing as an individual human.

PASSAGE 7

Unfolding Health of Being

Blessed are those who wash their robes, that they may have the right to the tree of life and may go through the gates into the city. Revelation 22:14 New International Version

Then Jesus said unto them, Verily, verily, I say unto you, Except ye eat the flesh of the Son of man, and drink his blood, ye have no life in you.

Whoso eateth my flesh, and drinketh my blood, hath eternal life; and I will raise him up at the last day. For my flesh is meat indeed, and my blood is drink indeed.

He that eateth my flesh, and drinketh my blood, dwelleth in me, and I in him.

As the living Father hath sent me, and I live by the Father: so he that eateth me, even he shall live by me.

This is that bread which came down from heaven: not as your fathers did eat manna, and are dead: he that eateth of this bread shall live for ever.

John 6:53-58 King James Version

While the journey of embodying our Divine nature in our human experience may be different for each of us, its three fundamental, complementary and co-creative passages of unfolding are common to us all - awakening out of separate consciousness into one Divine Being, expressing as all that is; unfolding one heart of Being – Divine, intelligent, unconditional Love; and, ultimately, unfolding Divine, immortal body of Life/Light.

As we awake into our original nature, Light of Being, and allow Light/Love of Being to metamorphose separate, emotional heart into one Divine heart of Being expressing as each unique human heart, Light/Love of Being flows from the heart down to the base of the spine, our root center, and begins spontaneously to metamorphose our mortal body into Divine immortal body of Life/Light.

This metamorphosis of personal biology, reflective of separate consciousness, into immortal body of Life/Light unfolds according to the same process that facilitates the metamorphosis personal mind and heart into Divine mind and heart. Just as Light of Being flows into our crown and heart center igniting mental and emotional energy signatures of separation into Divine mind and heart, so too it flows into our root center, igniting the biological energies, reflective of separate consciousness, into Divine immortal body of Life/Light.

Since each of our paths home from the suffering of separation into the wholeness of our Divine nature pass through different landscapes, we each accumulate unique energy distortions. Each of our energy centers become more or less silted up by our unique accumulation of mental, emotional and biological disharmonies, and their corresponding limiting thoughts, feelings, beliefs and sensations. Such silting diminishes and inhibits the power, purity and essential nature of Divine Presence flowing as River of Light through and as these centers; rendering each of us, in our own unique way, less able to embody, reflect and express our original nature.

How long it will take for humanity, as a whole, to awake out of the mental, emotional and biological pain of separation and metamorphose into the absolute wellbeing of our Divine nature depends on us. It depends on our willingness to surrender our experience of separate "I", separate heart and, ultimately, separate biology into the one Light/Love/Life of Being; on our willingness to allow the death and rebirth of who we think, feel, believe and experience our self, mind, heart and biology, to be.

As we have seen, when we resist the one Self that we are, perpetuating, instead, the consciousness of separation and suffering, we live disconnected from our limitless Divine nature. Like a goldfish in a glass bowl floating on the ocean, we swim around in our bowl, sustaining ourselves, to the best of our ability, with the nutrients accessible within our limited world. Our limited perspective blinds us to the realization that we could relinquish our limited experience and awake as limitless ocean of Being.

As we unfold the courage to surrender our small fishbowls of separate consciousness and awaken into our true nature, one Divine Presence, we spontaneously realize that, just as we cannot access Divine Presence and unconditional Love outside of us, so too we cannot find absolute health outside of us. We cannot attain it through medical interventions, pharmaceuticals, supplements, herbs, nutrition and exercise;

nor from stem cells or any other cutting-edge medical treatments.

We realize that, while natural and western medicine may be essential for the relative health and repair of our bodies as we awake from separate consciousness and its inevitable corollary biological degeneration, they are, ultimately, only crutches. We recognize that, while they may serve us during passages of our Divine unfolding, a time will come when we will live without them.

For now, we realize that health is not something we can pick from a tree, find in a bottle or develop in a gym, since, fundamentally, our body reflects who, consciously and unconsciously, we believe, think, feel and experience it to be more than what we put into it, do to it or prompt it to do. We understand that when we regularly inhabit separate consciousness our body will inevitably reflect this consciousness of limitation and separation. Habitually fed a diet of mental conflict and emotional suffering, it will express this conflict and suffering as disharmony, degeneration, disease and, ultimately, death.

We realize that biological degeneration and disease are, therefore, not the inevitable consequence of being human, but, instead, the inevitable result of separate consciousness that believes, among other things, that, while life may be extended with appropriate nutrition, exercise, psychological and spiritual practices, the body is a finite source of energy, a non-rechargeable battery. We realize there is, ultimately, no such thing as complete health separate from embodying Light/Love/Life of Being that we are; and conversely, there is no such thing as embodying Being without, ultimately, unfolding the experience of health. Since health is our Divine nature. Health is who we are.

We recognize that what we were conditioned by western medicine to consider as health is merely a distorted and limited reflection of our true nature, Life of Being. For western medicine teaches us to believe our bodies are healthy when our biological markers are in the normal range relative to the average markers of other seemingly healthy human populations. This definition of health does not allow for the unfolding of original health, the absolute health of our Divine nature. It simply measures the health of our bodies relative to other human bodies, as they all, inhabited by separate consciousness, move inexorably towards aging, disease and death.

As we awake and embody wholeness of Being, our body begins to unfold absolute mind, heart and body health rather than relative health. Absolute biological health is self-sustaining. No longer prey to degeneration, disease and death, absolute health is the health we humans forgot when we fell into separate consciousness. Absolute health, Life of Being, like mind and heart of Being, is never a victim of disharmony and disease. For Divine body of Life, as distinct from the biology born from separate consciousness, is no more vulnerable to catching the flu from a friend than heart of Being is vulnerable to catching anger or fear from another.[16]

---

[16] Some highly evolved humans consciously assume the disease of others. However, this is a conscious choice rather than a contagion. Sometimes, however, the rest of us may confuse empathy with compassion and, thereby, become porous to another's dis-ease or disease, since empathy allows us to experience what the other is experiencing. So, if it feels right,

As with each passage of our unfolding, as we unfold the absolute health of Life of Being it is important to avoid the temptation to compare. Comparisons not only perpetuate and strengthen the experience of separation, they also confuse and misguide us. For example, just because our body is sick while our friend's body seems healthy does not mean, necessarily, that we are holding onto and creating more toxic thoughts, beliefs and emotions than our friend, exercising less and eating less healthy foods. That might be the case, but it also might be the case that this is our time to embrace into consciousness more of the biological signatures of separation carried in and reflected by our cells.

Just as discernment is critical in the unfolding of the heart, allowing us to distinguish, for example, between the heart realizing its divine nature, unconditional Love and captured by ephemeral waves of romantic love, so, too, discernment is critical in the unfolding of Life of Being. We need to discern, for example, between the illusion that our body is metamorphosing into a body of Light whereas, in reality, we are merely disassociating from the body to protect ourselves from psychological wounds buried in our cells; denying emotions, feelings, sensations to hang out in some seemingly safe, ungrounded, transcendent state, and confusing this disembodied experience with body of light.

Discernment is also important in the experience of will. The will of separate consciousness may coopt the River of Light/Love/Life practice into its service. Ambitious for spiritual achievement, it may, for example, invoke more

---

to respond to another with empathy, we need to be conscious to avoid absorbing the other 's dis-ease.

powerful energies of Light than our body is currently able to integrate safely. So, instead of spontaneously refining and aligning with our Divine nature, Light/Love/Life of Being, our body "burns out", or, like a car injected with the wrong fuel, runs down rather than running better. Even when our body can tolerate the Light of a higher, more awake consciousness, an unhealed and, therefore, unready emotional body, blasted by too powerful a Light, too high a consciousness, can fracture, provoking breakdown rather than breakthrough, a psychotic episode rather than Divine heart unfolding. In all cases, when separate ego-consciousness interferes with the organic unfolding of our Divine nature, co-opting spontaneous passages of transformation in service to its own agenda and survival, our unfolding results in still-birth, rather than metamorphosis.

Awakening our first energy center, our root, is a precondition of experiencing and accepting these biological signatures of separate consciousness into the hearth of the heart, and, thereby, unfolding Divine wholeness and, as a result, Divine health. When the root center is distorted by the painful imprints of separate consciousness, River of Light is unable to flow through it permeating our biology with the Divine Life and aligning it with the blueprint of Divine body that is inherent in Life of Being.

A closed or constricted root center veils our experience of the unity of all Life - Life of individual body, Life of Earth body, Life of all existence. Disconnected from Earth, plants, rocks and all living things, we are disconnected from the joyful, vital, exuberant experience of Divine Life. Our body feels more like a separate entity inhabiting a separate Earth than a unique expression of the one Divine Life that we are.

Even though we may be unfolding mind and heart of Being, our experience of separation from all Life everywhere depletes the vitality of our individual body, promoting degeneration and disease.

Our current human biology, reflective of the limitation and disharmony of separate consciousness, operates like a relatively closed system. Each new cell of our current biology only imperfectly replicates the old cell, leading inevitably to degeneration. Whereas the "cells" of the unfolding Divine Body, reflective of limitless Light/Love/Life of Being, increasingly express the Divine human blueprint, the Light that we are.

When we are fully present in our body, and the Light of awareness is, thereby, able to permeate our cells, the Light unveils the sensations, signatures of separate consciousness, that our bodies carried for us while we were unable to register and acknowledge their pain. As we accept unconditionally these painful sensations into the hearth of our heart, we awaken to the Life body that permeates and enlivens our visible, tangible physical body. We realize this Life body as the one Life we share with all Life everywhere, a wave of the ocean of immortal Life, seamlessly one with It, and, thereby, eternally energized by It. Our root center tingles with quasi-erotic vitality. Our body relaxes into increasing harmony and wellbeing.

As our experience of our Divine Life body unfolds, our ability to feel and recognize the changing needs and conditions of our body increases, allowing us to know what it needs in each moment to support its unfolding within the chrysalis of becoming. To discern, for example, whether our current biological discomfort is due to a virus or is, instead, a symptom of a purification process integral to the body's healing, refinement and transformation.

Just as denial, resistance or repression of our emotional pain walls off our psychological wounds to the Divine flame of transformation in the hearth of the heart, similarly any denial, resistance or repression of our biological sensations walls off our Life and form of our biology to its healing in the hearth of the heart. Just as we may be tempted to avoid emotional pain through distraction, addiction and denial, we may, similarly, be tempted to avoid the pain buried in our cells.

So, just as unfolding Divine mind and heart, Light/Love of Being, usually takes time and practice to become established in our human experience, so too does unfolding into consciousness our Life body as a wave of the one immortal Life of Being. Indeed, due to the deeply unconscious nature of some of our cellular pain, it can often take more time.

As River of Light/Love/Life flows into our root center, permeating our cells, and we begin to register some of the physical sensations, reflective of separate consciousness, the intensity of the discomfort may shock us. Particularly when, after emerging from the dark nights of heart unfolding, we assume that the most intense pain of our unfolding is behind us.

As we become willing to accept unconditionally our painful biological signatures of separation, we embrace them as precious lost sheep; energies that, forgetting their true nature, co-created humanity's virtual reality of separation and suffering. We accept them unconditionally into the hearth of the heart and allow the Divine flame of Being to ignite them back into our Self, Light/Love/Life of Being.

Some of the more intense psychological wounds buried within our body, and reflected by the condition of our cells, are often those associated with early parenting experiences. When as infants, for example, we experience regular disharmony with our mother, or primary caretaker, we may learn to distrust, deny, dissociate from our body and, therefore, from the wisdom of our biological instincts. We may seek to control our body. We may become ungrounded; living somewhat out of our body, rather than fully inhabiting it, being wholly present within it. Instead of experiencing body and Earth as expressions and condensations of the one spirit that we are, we may perceive a split between mind and body, spirit and matter. Instead of trusting and listening to our instincts, we may rely on our minds to second guess our instincts knowing; and our bodies may reflect this distrust and disconnection with degeneration and disease.

As we allow River of Light/Love/Life to permeate our body, accept unconditionally each uncomfortable sensation into the hearth of our heart and awake to our Life body as a wave of the one ocean of Divine Life, we begin awakening to the nature of Life. We experience its Presence, limitless vitality, harmony, balance and wellbeing. We look at a plant and recognize the vitality and levity of Life that allows the plant to grow towards the sky as the same vitality and levity of life that allows our body to be stand alive on the Earth. Awakening to our physical body as a condensation of Divine Life, as water is a condensation of steam, we allow the final vestiges of spirit/matter duality consciousness to dissolve;

and our body to begin to purify, refine and unfold its wholeness - its Divine health.

The process whereby Light/Love/Life of Being permeates and enlightens human mind, heart and body, unfolding Divine mind, heart and, ultimately, Divine body of the new human, has its reflection in the science of photons. In an episode of Wisdom Teachings, on Gaia.com, David Wilcock describes studies conducted by the Russian scientist, Dr. Peter Gariaev using lasers to resurrect seeds killed by the Chernobyl nuclear disaster. According to David Wilcock, Dr. Gariaev first gathered a group of healthy seeds and shone a laser light onto them. He then took a group of the same kind of seeds that had been killed by the Chernobyl radiation and redirected onto them the same laser light that he had previously shone on the healthy seeds. The redirection of the laser light from the living seeds to the dead seeds resulted in the complete resurrection of the dead seeds.[17]

In another experiment that included unconscionable cruelty to rats, Dr. Gariaev subdivided a group of rats into two groups. He injected one group of rats with the toxin, alloxan, which destroyed the insulin-producing cells of the pancreas of each rat in this group. The rats all died within 4-6 days of receiving the injection. Dr. Gariaev gave the second group of rats the same dose of alloxan. Then he shone a laser through the spleen and pancreas of some healthy rats, and on the 4th day after the second group of rats received alloxan he redirected this same laser onto the poisoned rats. In a little over a week the spleens and pancreases of the majority of the poisoned rats who received the laser treatment completely

---

[17] *Healing with the Source Field 35* April 2012 *Gaia.com* David Wilcock

regrew. In other words, the template of a healthy spleen and pancreas, picked up by the laser and redirected onto the poisoned rats, enabled the majority of the poisoned rats to regrow their spleens and pancreases.

As we accept our physical body and allow Light/Love/Life of Being to permeate it, our bodies have similar potential to heal as the poisoned rats. Like the programmed laser healing the rats, Light of Being may spontaneously heal our biological dis-ease, reflective of separate consciousness, into wholeness and health. In time, it metamorphoses personal, corruptible body into the Divine Life body of the new human.

We need to remember, however, that each of us is unique, with different histories, psychological and spiritual experiences, as well as different life missions. So, each of our bodies needs its own time to metamorphose from mortal body into Divine immortal body of absolute health. Some of us, while embodying the wholeness that we are, Light/Love/Life of Being, may experience no significant improvement in biological health throughout a particular life. Others, awakening as and embodying Light/Love/Life of Being, may experience immediate health improvements. Then, later in life, encounter a health crisis that invites them deeper into the experience of body. Others of us, embodying Being may continue to enjoy relatively good physical health for the rest of our life.

As we begin awakening as Divine Life, we discover a new appreciation, respect and caring for the living being that is our body. We find ourselves feeling and touching it with fresh love and gratitude; with unfolding recognition of its Divinity. Listening more receptively and respectfully to its instinctual wisdom, we tenderly embrace it as the embryo it is, gestating within the chrysalis of its own unfolding. Honoring it as condensed Divine Light, we befriend it as a sacred expression of who we are, Divine consciousness. We appreciate it gifting us our Earth walk and our ability, thereby, to play our part in unfolding the new humanity.

Regardless of how our body feels each day, whether vital and exuberant or compromised by exhaustion and disease, we are grateful for its being. We cherish it. Aware that it hears and reflects back to us each of our thoughts, feelings, images and beliefs about it, we warmly appreciate its absolute health, even when our senses offer us less than healthy sensations. For, awake now as Light/Love/Life of Being, we are awake as the absolute health and harmony of who we are, even when our biology continues to reflect residues of separate consciousness.

Although we may listen to the advice of doctors, friends and natural healers, we allow our body friend the final say about which healing modalities, exercise programs, medical treatments, supplements and diets are appropriate during each passage of its metamorphosis. While we offer our body friend options, we listen to and trust that the spark of the Divine in each cell alone knows what our body needs in each moment of its unfolding. We distinguish between our chemical and emotional addictions and the body's authentic changing appetites. Regardless of how unusual the body's appetites may seem, we relinquish all food and exercise "religions" and trust and honor these appetites. Since now we recognize the authentic appetites of the body are similar to the authentic appetites of mind and heart – those inclinations and interests, uncontaminated by the distortions of separate consciousness, that unfold more of the health and wholeness that is our Divine nature.

Embodying the Light/Love/Life of Being spontaneously refines and sensitizes the relationship between consciousness and body. We lose the seemingly denser energetic insulation between mind, heart and body created by separate consciousness. We experience the biochemical reflections of consciousness and unconsciousness occurring more quickly than they did when we experienced spirit and matter, mind and body, and body and Earth as separate from each other.

Our biology becomes increasingly sensitive to our thoughts, emotions, images, beliefs and feelings; and not just our own. Since, until our consciousness stabilizes as Light/Love of Being, shining like the sun, our mental, emotional and physical bodies may become increasingly sponge-like; absorbing and reflecting not only more quickly and strongly our own fluctuating emotions and thoughts but also those of others. Therefore, we need to be vigilant around those moments when, slipping back into separate consciousness, we start to absorb and reflect duality consciousness. Aware of when our mind, heart and body are sponging up the discordant thoughts and emotions of separate consciousness, rather than allowing the harmony and wholeness of their Divine nature to shine.

When our awakening and embodying occurs spontaneously in Divine order and timing, the metamorphosis of mind, heart and biology unfold naturally, organically and gracefully. Even though residues of mental, emotional and biological energies, reflective of separate consciousness, may for a while continue to rise into consciousness expressing as the pain of ignorance, desire, conflict, fear and disease, the Divine Presence that we are increasingly permeates and, thereby, metamorphoses mind, heart and biology.

The more we unfold and live our true nature, Light/Love/Life of Being, the less banished we feel from paradise. Accounts of ancient, instinctual paradise gardens, when humans lived naturally in health and harmony with each other, nature and all existence, are not limited to the Bible. The ancient Chinese described a time when

"good men were not appreciated: ability was not conspicuous. Rulers were mere beacons, while the people were as free as the wild deer. They were upright without being conscious of duty to their neighbors. They loved one another without being conscious of charity. They were true without being conscious of loyalty. They were honest without being conscious of good faith. They acted freely in all things without recognizing obligations to anyone. Thus their deeds left no trace; their affairs were not handed down to posterity."[18]

"Primeval man enjoyed perfect tranquility throughout life. In his day the positive and negative principles were peacefully united; spiritual beings gave no trouble: the four seasons followed in due order; nothing suffered any injury; death was unknown; men had knowledge but no occasion to use it. This may be called perfection of unity....At that period, nothing was ever made so; but everything was so."[19]

"And so, in the days when natural instincts prevailed, men moved quietly and gazed steadily. At that time there were no roads over mountains, nor boats, nor bridges over water. All things were

---

[18] *Chuang Tzu* translated by H.A. Giles *p. 1.*
[19] ibid, p 156.

produced, each for its own proper sphere. Birds and beasts multiplied. Trees and shrubs grew up. The former might be led by the hand; you could climb up and peep into the raven's nest. For then man dwelt with birds and beasts, and all creation was one. There were no distinctions of good and bad men. Being all equally without knowledge, their virtue could not go astray. Being all equally without evil desires, they were in a state of natural integrity, the perfection of human existence."[20]

As our Earth and solar system are increasingly graced by the Light of unity consciousness, and separate consciousness is, therefore, no longer supported by the energy fields it inhabits, it becomes easier to realize our Divine nature. As the metamorphosis of mind, heart and, ultimately, body occurs, we cease to experience River of Light/Love/Life as a practice, and realize, instead, that River of Light is who we are. Embodying River of Light/Love/Life - Divine mind, heart and Life, we become the new human Divine **Being.**

---

[20] ibid. p. 9

Meditative Play: Unfolding Health of Being

Summary of Passage 7

As we allow Light/Love of Being to flow into our root center and accept into the hearth of our heart each experience of our body, we not only awake as Life of Being, absolute Divine health, but Life of Being now begins to metamorphose our physical body into Divine body, just as Light of Being metamorphoses separate, emotional "heart" into Divine heart. As we embody Light/Love/Life of Being, we unfold the health and wholeness of the new human.

If it feels appropriate, ask Divine Self and your spirit guides to enhance, facilitate, unfold and illuminate your meditative experience.

1. Become aware of Light of Being, Divine Presence, in between your thoughts, emotions and sensations.

2. Surrender the experience of being a separate identity into Light of I Am – not separate I, but Light of I AM, Light of Being.

3. If you notice consciousness contracting back into separation by identifying with a thought, image, emotion or sensation, relax back into Light of Being, accepting each experience as it is.

4. Allow Light/Love of Being to flow into your root center, and experience your root center expressing Light/Love of Being as immortal Life of Being.

5. Experience Life of Being.

6. Remaining fully present in your physical body, allow your awareness to flow through each part of your body, unconditionally accepting each sensation into the hearth of your heart.

7. Accept each sensation in the hearth of the heart as it is, for as long as it is.

8. Experience the absolute health and vitality of Divine Life flowing through and as each cell in your body.

9. Experience your individual body as a wave of the limitless ocean of Divine Life, Divine health.

10. Experience Light/Love/Life of I Am, Divine Presence, expressing as Divine mind, heart and body of your new humanity.

PASSAGE 8

Body of Light

"If thine eye be single, then the whole body shall be full of light."

Matthew 6:22 King James Version

"Now Mary stood outside the tomb crying. As she wept, she bent over to look into the tomb and saw two angels in white, seated where Jesus' body had been, one at the head and the other at the foot. They asked her, "Woman, why are you crying?"

"They have taken my Lord away," she said, "and I don't know where they have put him." At this, she turned around and saw Jesus standing there, but she did not realize that it was Jesus. He asked her, "Woman, why are you crying? Who is it you are looking for?"

Thinking he was the gardener, she said, "Sir, if you have carried him away, tell me where you have put him, and I will get him."

Jesus said to her, "Mary."

She turned toward him and cried out in Aramaic, "Rabboni!" (which means "Teacher")."

John 20:11-18 New International Version

L ike the caterpillar dissolving its caterpillar nature in the chrysalis to unfold its butterfly nature, our current human nature, including our physical body, may move into its own chrysalis and metamorphose not only into Divine mind and heart but into immortal body of Light/Life.

As we relinquish the experience of inhabiting a separate physical body, and awake as Life of Being our experience of inhabiting a degenerating body, a non-rechargeable battery, begins to transform into the experience of being Divine Life expressing as an individual life body. Since Divine Life, like the sun, is simultaneously and inseparably Divine Love and Light, Divine Life body is simultaneously immortal body of Light, capable of expressing as an individual body of Light. The same immortal body of Life/Light unfolded by Jesus through his resurrection and ascension, as well by others in other cultures.

Just as the metamorphosis of personal mind and heart into Divine mind and heart is usually a gradual process, so too is the metamorphosis of our corruptible body into immortal body of Life/Light. However, unlike the caterpillar that is completely immobilized within the chrysalis, we may continue, to a lesser or greater extent, to live functional lives during each of our three passages of metamorphosis - mind, heart and biology. Though some of us may require extensive rest and solitude during certain times.

As our corruptible biological body, reflective of separate consciousness, is permeated and enlightened by Light/Love/Life of Being, unfolding more of the health and wholeness of our Divine nature, its energy gradually refines. Like steam heated into air, our corruptible body, ignited by the flame of Being, evaporates into immortal body of Life/Love/Light.

Since the symbolism of the Light of Being dream, described in *Passage 2*, offers a window into the nature and experience of immortal body of Life/Light, here is a review of part of the dream so that the images, as icons, may carry us through them into direct experience.

I dream of *a man whom I have met a few times. As I am present with him, undisturbed by emotions or thoughts, I experience his body dissolving into a brilliant "star" of clear Light/Love and immortal Life. My body also dissolves into an identical "star" of clear Light/Love/Life. Now our male and female natures remember their wholeness, their androgyny. Like two flames in close proximity to each other, we ignite into one flame. Our one flame of Being spontaneously awakes as Source of all experience, Light/Love/Life of Being, Divine Presence, Oneness.*

As Light of Being, I Am home. I Am whole - limitless, eternal potential. I Am Light/ Love and immortal Life. I am Divine Presence, Oneness expressing as all that is, as all levels of consciousness and experience - mineral, plant, animal, human, galactic and cosmic. I Am One and the many unique faces of One. I Am bliss of Being doing nothing, being no one, going nowhere.

"Now that you are awakening out of the illusion of separation into the truth of the one Being," says Light of Being in the wordless language of Light, "You need to return to Earth. As a human you need to embody Light, Love and immortal Life of Being."

The dream reflects both the potential for our corruptible body to metamorphose into Divine, immortal body of Light/Life as well as for immortal body of Light to condense into the experience of an individual human body. It reflects the infinite potential of Being to express as different levels of consciousness, energetic densities and forms.

The whole embodiment of Light/Love/Life of Being, the metamorphosis not only of separate "I" mind and heart, but also separate "I" body into Divine mind, heart and body of Light is, perhaps, our ultimate act of Love as evolving humans. By way of it we transcend not only all personal suffering but all personal pain, including the pain of biological degeneration, disease and death. Since humanity is one being, when any one of us unfolds Divine mind, heart and body we facilitate this whole embodiment of Being in every human; and, thereby, facilitate the whole of humanity's liberation from both suffering and pain.

My first glimpse of Divine body of Life/Light arrived over thirty years ago, during a visit to Florence, Italy with my teenage daughter. One morning she and I walked from our hotel to the Monastery of San Marco where Fra Angelico created some of his most famous frescoes including the Annunciation. It was a cold December day. The monastery was not heated and we were not dressed for freezing temperatures. The biting cold radiated from the thick, stone walls. We were alone. Other tourists were probably deterred by the icy weather. I empathized with them, but we were only in Florence for a few days, and I was eager to see all the small monastic cells, each graced by a different Fra Angelico fresco. However, the physical discomfort of the cold was somewhat dulling my receptivity to the beauty of this fifteenth-century painter.

By the time I reached the sixth cell, I was moving fast, eagerly anticipating the warmth of our hotel room. My daughter, physically bolder than I, was still admiring the fresco of the Annunciation at the entrance of the monastery when I pushed open the arched wooden door of the sixth whitewashed cell. The pale winter light shone in through the high window gently illuminating the small space. I found myself in front of the fresco of the *Transfiguration*. Instantly my consciousness was elevated into a world inaccessible to cold. I did not notice the artistic skill of the fresco depicting the transfigured Jesus appearing to his disciples. Neither did I notice the cracked and fading paint. In that timeless moment, there was only Jesus awake as "Christ" consciousness expressing as immortal body of Life/Light.

The radiance of transfigured Christ consciousness once again elevated my consciousness out of the experience of duality into our original nature – Light of I Am. Moreover, this time the veil of separation obscuring our true nature dissolved enough not only to reveal our Divine Self but also to reveal the Divine potential of every human body. I realized what I was being shown was not something unique to Jesus, but rather our human birthright. I saw how embodying our Divine nature not only metamorphoses personal mind and heart into Divine mind and heart but also, ultimately, our corruptible biology into Divine, immortal body of Life/Light. I realized that the transfiguration of Jesus unfolded spontaneously as he relinquished the final signatures of separate consciousness at every level of his human experience, mind, heart and body, thereby revealing to the rest of us our Divine potential and destiny – our Divine humanity.

Initially, when I contemplated this initiatory experience in cell six of the monastery of San Marco, it seemed that the transfiguration of Jesus' mortal body into immortal body of Life/Light suggested that each human has the potential for unfolding, experiencing and inhabiting an individual body of Life/Light. However, I soon realized that this perception was limited by the lens of separate consciousness. It soon became clear that our immortal body of Life/Light is not, essentially, an individual body. While it can, when appropriate, express as an individual body of Life/Light, its essential nature is eternally and indivisibly one Divine body of Life/Light. Just as the one Being that we are may express its Self as the experience of an individual human being, like the ocean expressing as an individual wave, it may also express as the experience of an individual body of Life/Light. While its absolute nature is eternally and indivisibly one. One Divine Being - one Divine mind and heart, and one immortal body of Life/Light.

While some believe that the resurrection of Jesus, along with every other aspect of his nature, is unique to Jesus, Jesus himself says *"he that believeth on me, the works that I do shall he do also; and greater works than these shall he do; because I go unto my Father."*[21]

With these words, Jesus acknowledges that each of us, not only him, can awake and embody our Divine nature, for each of us is not only born from but inseparable from Divine consciousness. Jesus simply shows us the way. His example invites and inspires us all not only to awake as Christ consciousness, Light/Love/Life of Being, but to embody wholly our Divine nature so we not only unfold Divine mind and heart but also, ultimately, Divine body of Life/Light.

Our human potential to unfold the immortal body of Life/Light is also recognized, honored and taught by other spiritual traditions. Each, in their way, acknowledges that our current human nature is only a pupal form of our true human nature; our current biology only a pupal form of our Divine immortal body of Life/Light.

The Dzogchen tradition of Tibetan Buddhism, for example, contains highly refined and proven teachings for the unfolding of immortal body of Life/Light. It teaches that, within our Buddha nature, immortal body of Life/Light already exists, and, therefore, needs no unfolding, for it is always present and perfect. Dzogchen recognizes that it is,

[21] John 14:12 King James Version

therefore, only from the relative perspective of evolving human consciousness that we can talk about unfolding immortal body of Life/Light, or, indeed, unfolding any other experience of our original Divine nature.

Like some other spiritual teachings, Dzogchen uses the image of a mirror to describe our original nature which it understands as pure awareness, primordial purity. It teaches that, while the mirror has the capacity to reflect whatever is in front of it, the nature of the mirror is never obscured, distorted or impacted by the reflection. It is always the same; beyond time and space, pure, unflawed, absolute perfection, regardless of what it reflects. Dzogchen acknowledges that our Divine nature, symbolized by the mirror, cannot be described in human language. For human language, as we have seen, reflects the experience of space/time, and includes thoughts and concepts which inevitably reflect the experience of difference and relativity. Whereas Divine consciousness transcends and includes all experience of space/time, including all thoughts, concepts, feelings and sensations – all experience of seeming similarity, relativity and difference. It just is – absolute, pristine Being.

The Dzogchen practitioner recognizes that our experience of a personal biological body, like our experience of a personal mental and emotional body, merely expresses separate consciousness. She, therefore, allows not only personal mind and heart but also, ultimately, personal body to dissolve into the one absolute Divine reality that we are; to metamorphose into the primordial energetic essence of the Five Pure Lights, known, in Dzogchen, as Rainbow Body - Divine, immortal body of Light.

Dzogchen recognizes two principal ways of unfolding Rainbow Body. The more common way includes the familiar death experience, during which the practitioner's body gradually shrinks after death while emanating rainbow light. After several days, provided the body is left untouched, all that remains of the corpse is either a small figurine, or merely hair and nails. According to David Wilcock, in his discussion of Rainbow Body on Gaiatv, there are at least one hundred and sixty thousand documented cases of Rainbow Body in Tibet, India and China alone.[22]

The Tibetan Buddhist teacher, Sogyal Rinpoche, in his book, *The Tibetan Book of Living and Dying,* offers his personal account of the father of his tutor, Sonam Namgal, realizing Rainbow Body by way of the death process. At the time Sogyal Rinpoche was a young man living in a Tibetan monastery.

"In 1952 there was a famous instance of the rainbow body in the East of Tibet, witnessed by many people.

"He was a very simple, humble person, who made his way as an itinerant stone carver, carving mantras and sacred texts. Some say he had been a hunter in his youth and had received teaching from a great master. No one really knew he was a practitioner; he was truly called 'a hidden yogin'."

". . . he then fell ill, or seemed to, but became strangely, increasingly happy. When the illness got worse, his family called in masters and doctors. His son told him he should remember all the teachings he had heard, and he smiled and said "I have forgotten

[22] *The Rainbow Body* David Wilcock, *Wisdom Teachings, Season 1, Episode 10, February 2013*

them all and, anyway, there is nothing to remember. Everything is illusion, but I am confident that all is well.

"*Just before his death at seventy-nine, he said "All I ask is that when I die, don't move my body for a week." When he died his family wrapped his body and invited Lamas and monks to come and practice for him. They placed the body in a small room in the house, and they could not help noticing that although he had been a tall person, they had no trouble getting it in, as if he were becoming smaller. At the same time, an extraordinary display of rainbow-colored light was seen all around the house. When they looked into the room on the sixth day, they saw that the body was getting smaller and smaller. On the eighth day after his death, the morning in which the funeral had been arranged, the undertakers arrived to collect the body. When they undid its coverings, they found nothing inside but his nails and hair.*"[23]

The second, rarer way, of realizing Rainbow Body, attained by only a few exceptionally enlightened practitioners, occurs without passing through the experience of biological death. It is known in Dzogchen as the Great Transference. The Tibetan Buddhist master of the eighth century, Padmasambhava, founder of the Nyingma school of Tibetan Buddhism is reported to have attained Rainbow Body in this way.

The Zanglingma autobiography says that after giving his final instructions, "*Padmasambhava mounted a beam of sunlight and in the flicker of a moment soared away into the open sky. From the direction of the south west, he turned his face to look back, and sent forth a light ray of immeasurable loving kindness that established the disciples in the state of non-return. Accompanied by a cloud-like throng of dakinis, outer and inner, and amid the sound*

---

[23] *Tibetan Book of Living & Dying* Sogyal Rinpoche, Harper San Francisco 1994 Chapter 10 pp 168

of the music they were offering, he went to the south-western continent of Ngayab."[24]

Accounts of the unfolding of our immortal body of Life/Light, without passing through death, are not limited to Tibetan Buddhism. For example, Swami Ramalingam, a nineteenth-century, enlightened Indian is also reported to have transmuted his body into Light without passing through biological death. Moreover, prior to unfolding his body of Light, Swami Ramalingam was reported also to have unfolded the "perfect" body, the body of perfect health - Divine Life body.

"Swami Ramalingam, popularly known as Vallalar, was one of the most notable saints on the Indian sub-continent during the 19th century. He was born on October 5, 1823, in Marudur near Chidambaram into a Hindu Saivite family, the fifth child and last son of his father Ramayya Pillai and mother Chinnammayyar. It is said she had borne him in her womb after she received Vibhuti, the sacred ash of blessings from an unknown guest of honor, a Siva Yogi who blessed her with a son like himself. Vallalar left the world on January 30, 1874 at age 51. When he was only six months old his father died and Ramalinga was brought up under the auspices and tutelage of his elder brother, who, it has been said, had a good working knowledge of things religious.

"At the age of 27, he was married to one Danammal. Marital life did not distract him from his religious duty. As an ardent follower of bhakti (the practice of devotional worship) he was a relentless critic of practice based on birth, class, status or privilege. He had no regard for the 'Puranas', 'Vedas', and the 'Agamas'. He worshiped God as Light (Jothi) and was a man of utmost love and compassion

---

[24] www.rigpawiki.org

for all living creatures. It is said that he would weep at the sight of even a withering crop. He firmly believed in anna dana, the free offering of food to the needy....

"It can be seen from the history of his life that in his later years his physical body had become tenuous and translucent. Disciples have recorded that it cast no distinct shadow. It is said that several attempts were made to photograph him, but since light passed through his body no clear image could be obtained. What could be seen were only his clothing and a very misty vision of his face and limbs, and from such a translucent body made so by pure living, dematerialization was but a few steps away.

"Swami Ramalingam (Vallalar) says, "Life of eternal bliss is union with God. Those who have achieved this will have transmuted this impure carnal body into a pure golden body and again have the pure body transformed into super sensible, spiritual body"....

"Spirituality that secluded itself from the common people had no meaning for Swami Ramalingam (Vallalar). His God-consciousness was based on love and compassion. As already seen, he was never at peace when people went without food. What was the meaning of kindness and love if one did not satisfy the hunger of a fellow human being? Moreover, food was the basic need of the body and body was the seat of the soul. Without taking care of the body how could anyone take care of the soul that dwelt in the body? Thus the very basis of spirituality was, according to Swamiji, the removal of hunger, since removal of hunger meant renovation of the living temple of God....

"The saint told his disciples that he was in the last days of his physical existence and that he would soon pass into the astral world. He then secluded himself in final preparation.

The news that the saint had locked himself up in a room became known. There was much excitement because the saint had earlier been talking about the possibility of the living dissolution of his physical body. Many people believed him and now they knew the final days had come.

"Three months after he locked the door to his room, the news eventually reached the government at Madras. Some officials came to investigate. They ordered the door to be opened. To the great wonder and amazement of all that stood around, they found no one inside the room. A thorough inspection of the whole building was made and nothing suspicious could be found. The officials questioned the disciples and found them to be very simple and innocent people. Now it was clear that, as proclaimed, the saint had achieved the unachievable: without discarding his physical body, he had dematerialized.

"The life and writings of Saint Ramalingam (Vallalar) have evidence enough to support dematerialization. They make it clear to us that the swami had been preparing all his life for this final achievement. He had been telling his followers that he would pass into eternal life, not by shedding his physical body, but by changing it into a subtle, invisible, deathless body. There are frequent references in his poems first to the hope and then to the certainty of his union with God by means of acquiring a wonderful, celestial body that would be beyond death or destruction."

Swami Ramalingam used to pray "Lord, take this body of mine and my spirit in exchange for your body and your spirit to enable this very body of flesh to become a body of light... transmuting this body of skin and bones, I shine with a golden form you have given me a form perpetual which nothing can destroy… grace, knowledge, love and an indestructible body these have been your gifts to me."[25]

The Old Testament also contains ascension stories. Elijah is described as ascending without passing through physical death.

"And it came to pass, as they still went on, and talked, that, behold, there appeared a chariot of fire, and horses of fire, and parted them both asunder; and Elijah went up by a whirlwind into heaven."[26]

According to John White, *"In the Christian tradition (the body of Light)…. is called "the resurrection body" or "the glorified body." St. Paul called it "the celestial body" or "spiritual body. "In Sufism it is called "the most sacred body" (wujud al-aqdas).In Taoism it is called "the diamond body," and those who have attained it are called "the immortals" and "the cloudwalkers. In Tibetan Buddhism it is called "the light body. "In some mystery schools it is called "the solar body. In Rosicrucianism it is called "the diamond body of the temple of God." In Tantrism and yoga it is called the "the vajra body," "the adamantine body" and "the divine body. In Vedanta it is called "the superconductive body." In Kriya yoga it is called "the body of bliss. In Gnosticism and Neoplatonism it is called "the radiant body. In the alchemical tradition, it is called "the glory of the whole universe" or the "golden body. In the Hermetic Corpus it is called "the immortal body" (soma athanaton). In ancient Egypt it was called the Ankh. In Old Persia it was called "the indwelling divine potential" (fravashi or fravarti). In the Mithraic liturgy it was called "the perfect body" (soma teleion). In the philosophy of Sri*

---

[25] https://pranashakty.org/jothi/about-swami-ramalingam/
[26] 2 Kings 2:11 King James Version

Aurobindo it is called "the Divine Body," composed of supramental substance."[27]

There is at least one 20th century western account of an early stage of the unfolding of immortal body of Life/Light. It is reported by Ricardo Bandini in his book, Posito Super Virtutibus. Ricardo describes how in the summer of 1930 during a visit to Assisi, Italy *"At the Sacro Convento of Saint Francis I ran into a...Franciscan, a rather tall fellow with a beard, nice looking...Seeing that he wore a beard I imagined he was a missionary, something I had desired but which problems with my eyes had made impossible. I asked him if he worked in the missions and he replied affirmatively and introduced himself as Father Maximillan Kolbe. He conversed with me about the Madonna.....Speaking...with great enthusiasm, he became, as I watched transfigured, in a diaphanous form, almost transparent, and surrounded by a halo of light, all of which lasted while he spoke......I found myself trembling with a sort of fear, filled with confusion – so moved that tears came out my eyes."*[28]

As we have seen, the precondition of the metamorphosis of personal mental, emotional and biological body into Divine mind, heart and body is the realization that we are already are all that is; that there is, in other words, no outside. Just as we only look within to unfold Divine mind and heart, so, too, we only look within to unfold Divine body. Surrendering the experience of body as a separate entity, reflective of separate consciousness and, therefore, running on a finite battery of

---

[27] *Resurrection and the Body of Light* John White, Quest 97. 1 (Fall 2009) pp 11-15
[28] Recounted by Mitchell Earl Gibson in *The Human Body of Light* Tybro Publications, 2009 p. 100

life force, we awake as immortal Light/Love/Life of Being, capable of expressing as an individual body of Light/Life.

Regardless of whether the unfolding of our Divine nature, our journey home, begins with awakening as Light of Being, or with the awakening as heart of Being, it is only after awakening at both levels, mind and heart, that our Divine nature can sufficiently permeate our cells for our biological experience to begin to metamorphose into Divine body of Life/Light. For, until the awakening of our Divine mind and heart is well underway, we regularly, as we mentioned, imprint our biology with thoughts and emotions reflective of separate consciousness, and, thereby, create a biology of disease, degeneration and death.

As our awakening as Light/Love of Being stabilizes, some of us may find ourselves confronted with intense physical challenges. After years of embodying Light/Love of Being and experiencing relatively good health, we may awake one morning confronted with a life-threatening disease. Our disease may reflect an accumulation of environmental toxins, residual unhealed psychological wounds, limiting thoughts, negative emotions, or even an unconscious absorption of a friend's mental, emotional or biological pain. When we embrace rather than resist the experience of our biological disease, allowing awareness to permeate our cells, our loving acceptance may not only heal the disease but also awaken us to body as an inseparable wave of Life of Being; and, thereby, quicken our awareness of the body's potential to metamorphose into Divine body of Life/Light.

Only the dualistic perspective of separate ego-consciousness, with its propensity to judge, might regard a life challenge, mental, emotional and biological, as a reflection of a mistake. Our original nature, Divine consciousness, like the sky, simply allows and accepts each passing storm, neither judging, resisting, denying or attempting to fix the passing storms. It perceives no mistakes.

Although it may be a while before most of us unfold Divine mind and heart, and considerably longer before we unfold Divine body/immortal body of Light/Life, each time we open to and resonate with the truth of who we are, we fertilize our unfolding, since truths are creative, living energies that naturally transform our consciousness and, thereby, our perception and experience.

When, for example, C.G. Jung, in the first half of the twentieth century, introduced into western psychology the truth of psychological projection – the tendency to perceive in others those qualities, negative or positive, that exist, consciously or unconsciously, within our self, this idea, rooted in the mirroring nature of reality, was confusing to many. Most of us, at least in Western cultures, were accustomed to believing that when we experienced, for example, anger in another person, and were ourselves emotionally triggered by this perception of anger, our emotional reaction was caused by the other. We assumed that our emotional reaction to our perception of another's anger had nothing to do with the possibility that we might carry within us some unacknowledged anger and everything to do with the other.

As Jung's concept of psychological projection seeped into mainstream western culture, increasingly showing up, in the second half of the twentieth century, in movies, books and TV shows, more and more of us began to explore the possibility that each emotion that we perceive in another and are emotionally triggered by, including anger, may reflect our own unacknowledged anger or anger related psychological wounds. Gradually many of us have been transformed by the experience of acknowledging our own anger rather than reacting to our perception of another's anger.

As we awake to the truth that consciousness, including unconsciousness, determines perception, we recognize that while, in each second, our brain receives billions of pieces of information, it is our unique mix of consciousness and unconsciousness that determines the approximately one percent of these we register, perceive, react and respond to. We recognize that when, for example, we experience a door as solid this does not tell us anything about the real nature of the door. It simply tells us something about the nature of sense-perceptible consciousness, the nature of our sense-perceptible experience. As our consciousness unfolds and refines our experience of the door transforms. Instead of merely experiencing the door as solid, we may also experience it as patterns of energy, waves of light. Moreover, we may realize that these waves of light are our original nature, Light of Being, expressing as the energy patterns our senses experience as a door.

As we acknowledge and accept responsibility for our experience, including our psychological projections, accepting within us that which we used to judge in others, and embracing the discomfort at the root of all emotional reaction, our heart, as we saw, spontaneously unfolds and stabilizes more of its Divine nature. We may experience a strengthening of the attributes of the heart, like compassion, kindness and equanimity, increasing awareness of the guidance of the heart as well as more frequent experiences of the essential nature of the heart. Now, not just in occasional, silent meditative moments, but increasingly amidst the chaos and busyness of our lives, we are awakening as Love. We are living Love.

As the truth and understanding of psychological projection percolates into collective consciousness, it is quickening the unfolding of Love in more and more of us, and, thereby, transforming our relationship with ourselves, with each other and all existence. Such is the power of a truth whose time has arrived. Divine body of Life/Light is another truth whose time has arrived to be seeded into human consciousness; not only to inspire us to open to its unfolding but, since biology reflects mind and heart, to quicken and nourish its unfolding.

As more of us hear the invitation to allow corruptible body to metamorphose into Divine body of Life/Light, its realization will cease to be the exclusive domain of a few ascended masters, like Jesus Christ, Padmasambhava and Swami Ramalingam. Instead, it will gradually become acknowledged and embraced as an integral expression of who we are. Like the idea of psychological projection, the truth of Divine body of Life/Light will, in time, percolate down from rarefied esoteric teachings into collective consciousness, transforming our understanding and, ultimately our experience of human nature, including human biology.

Although the invitation to us all in this time is not to believe in the idea of the body of Life/Light, but, instead, to open to direct experience, there are moments in our journey home during which belief can act as bridge to direct experience; a stepping stone allowing awareness to cross the river from belief/disbelief into insight. From the arrogance of the shuttered mind and heart, convinced that the dualistic experience of space/time is absolute reality, belief in the Divine, for example, can elevate consciousness into devotion to the Divine. In time devotion can heal and transform our emotional bodies, facilitating the metamorphosis of personal, emotional heart into Divine heart.

However, belief can also prevent the unfolding of our true nature. Since belief barricades the door to conscious experience of that which we believe. When we believe in something our belief implies we do not experience that in which we believe. For example, if we believe in angels, our belief suggests we have not experienced the beings we call angels. Once we do experience angels, we no longer believe in them.

So, rather than getting stuck on the bridge of belief, it is useful to recognize when it has carried us as far as it goes, and step off the other side into the humility of unknowing, embracing our sacred questions until they attract their answers. For example, if we cling to belief in our Divine nature we inevitably perpetuate the experience of separation from our Divine nature. When we relinquish this belief, we can venture into the cloud of unknowing. Released from the emotional security of belief, the security of having the answer to who we are, we can carry the question until the receptivity inherent in every authentic act of questioning unfolds our true nature.

A few years after the vision of the transfiguration of Jesus in front of Fra Angelico's fresco in Florence, I experienced myself, momentarily, inhabiting an individual expression of immortal body of Life/Light.

I awoke in the middle of the night from what seemed, at first, to be a dream of myself living in a community of Light beings. Once completely awake, I realized with astonishment that I was still living in this community of Light beings, inhabiting a radiant, somewhat fluid, translucent individual "body" of Life/Light that was simultaneously the Light/Love/Life of Being.

While awake as Light/Love/Life of Being, expressing as an individual body of Life/Light, I was also aware of having a human biological body on Earth. However, I was not able to experience this human body.

I noticed that my individual body of Light/Life had a translucent soft, radiant "head" and "face", but no permanent torso or limbs. I realized that, instead of expressing as a constant form, this body of Light could express as different patterns and densities of Light, according to the highest good. For example, it could condense into translucent "arms" and "legs" when arms and legs were needed for a certain experience. As soon as they were no longer needed, it could dematerialize them, dissolving them back into the limitless potential of Light/Life.

Awake as Light of Being expressing as an individual body of Light as well as a human biological body, I began to wonder about my human body. Suddenly both my human body and the Earth seemed far away, even unreachable. Frightened that I might not be able to get back into my human body, I instantly found myself back in it, lying in bed under my peach flannel comforter with my dog, Braveheart, asleep at my feet.

Instead of accepting the fear of disconnection from my human body into the hearth of the heart where it could be transmuted by Love into Love, my consciousness collapsed into fear. By identifying with the fear, experiencing myself in that moment as nothing but the fear of disconnection from my human body, my consciousness condensed into duality consciousness; and duality consciousness can only experience a corruptible biological body.

Since our nature is simultaneously One and each unique face of One, both ocean and wave, we can enjoy our sense-perceptible experience as well as many subtler levels of existence, inaccessible to our five senses. Provided we do not collapse consciousness into the experience of separation by identifying with any one expression of Being, we can relate to other humans, animals and nature as well as to other supersensible beings, outside the laws of space/time. We can inhabit our human biological body as well as different, subtler bodies, while remaining awake as the one undifferentiated Divine Being. If, during the community of light beings experience, I had been awake to our Divine nature my consciousness would not have collapsed into separation, into the either/or experience. Instead, as the one Light of Being, I would have continued to experience living within the community of Light beings in a body of Light/Life, capable of materializing and dematerializing, while, simultaneously, experienced living in my human, physical body.

While we might confuse the early stages of the metamorphosis of corruptible body into immortal body of Life/Light with biological death, the two are essentially different. The process of metamorphosis from mortal into immortal body is analogous to a flaming candle. When the candle flame goes out, and, therefore, ceases to melt the wax, the wax, like the biological body, is subject to the laws of entropy. It exists until it disintegrates. Whereas, when the candle flame continues to burn, devouring all the candle wax, the whole candle metamorphoses into the warmth, light and life of the flame. No wax is left behind subject to the laws of entropy. Similarly, during biological metamorphosis, the body, instead of disintegrating and returning its elements to the Earth by way of death, refines and, ultimately, metamorphoses into its original, nature, Divine Light.

During this process of metamorphosis, we cease to experience the body as an object, instrument, or even merely as a temple or servant of Divine Self. For now, regardless of any current biological challenges, we experience all physical things, including the human body and the Earth, as condensations of our Divine nature, Light of Being. We recognize the potential of Light/Life of Being both to condense into the experience of individual biology as well as to metamorphose back into Light, without going through the familiar human death process.

While some of us may recognize the idea of metamorphosing into Light as not only an idea whose time has come but a spiritual imperative for human wellbeing, others, when hearing about our corruptible biology metamorphosing into Light, may resonate with the caterpillar who, on seeing the butterfly, says "you won't get me up in one of those".

We humans have inhabited our caterpillar bodies for eons. Most of us have assumed that disease, degeneration and death are natural and appropriate, our only biological destiny. We have dismissed religious and spiritual accounts of ascension from mortal to immortal body of Life/Light as meaningless myths. We have confined our understanding of awakening out of separate consciousness into the Oneness that we are, Divine Presence, to our mind and heart, omitting our biology.

Since biological degeneration and death have been the usual experience for most of us throughout recorded history, we have confused the usual with the natural. We have confused our habitual experience of the body with the essential nature of the body. Just as it has been our usual experience to identify with and, thereby, suffer the illusion and pain of separate consciousness, so, too it has been our usual experience to get sick and die. However, patterns of being, experience and belief are not, as we have discussed, absolute truths of who we are. They are just perceptions and experiences of who we believe, think, imagine, feel and sense our self to be.

When we believe in the virtual reality of separation, we believe in and, therefore, identify with limitation in all forms and at all levels of existence. We identify with limitation of wisdom, creativity, love, abundance, vitality, health and so on. However, when we glimpse or, at least, intuit our true Divine nature, and awake to the truth that nothing is separate, and, therefore, nothing is disconnected from limitless potential of Being, including us and our bodies, we awake as our limitless, creative Divine potential.

As Divine creators who ventured into the play of separation and suffering, we humans, collectively and individually, are responsible for our life. We are responsible for who we experience our self to be, as well as for the life we live; responsible for every thought, feeling, attitude, creation, conscious and unconscious attitude and belief. Each creation that is out of alignment with the truth of being is, therefore, ours to gather back into the hearth of the heart wherein the flame of love transmutes it back into its Self - Light/Love/Life of Being.

We began birthing these corruptible bodies the moment we forgot our original nature and fell out of paradise into the experience of separation. Now, as we awake out of this virtual reality of separation, and embody who we are, we redeem emotional pain through the metamorphosis of emotional body into heart of Love, and biological pain through metamorphosis of corruptible biological body into Divine body of Life/Light.

Each time any one of us unfolds who we are, one Being, his/her awakening consciousness is the Light shining in the darkness of the virtual reality of separation. Like a flame in a dark cave, this darkness cannot ultimately withstand the power of Light. When a critical mass of us humans awakes and embodies who we are, Light/Love/Life of Being, the whole of humanity awakes and embodies our Divine nature. As this happens humanity leaves behind not only all existential and emotional pain and suffering, but also all degeneration, disease and death – all physical pain.

PASSAGE 9

Unfolding Body of Light

"The light of the body is the eye: if therefore thine eye be single, thy whole body shall be full of light."
Matthew 6:22-23 King James Bible

Jesus said *"Is it not written in your law, I said, Ye are gods?*
John 10:34 King James Bible

"The disciples said to Jesus, "Tell us how our end will be." Jesus said, "Have you discovered, then, the beginning, that you look for the end? For where the beginning is, there will the end be. Blessed is he who will take his place in the beginning; he will know the end and will not experience death."
The Gospel of Thomas 18, translated by Lambdin

When we awake as Divine consciousness, we find liberation from the pain of separation from our true identity, Light of I Am. However, as long as our heart sleeps to its Divine nature, we continue to experience psychological pain. This pain is often poignantly visible in those whose eyes radiate the beauty of awakening consciousness, but whose hearts remain constricted and distorted by unhealed psychological wounds and their expression as fears, desires and emotional attachments.

As we awake as Divine consciousness, as well as Divine heart of unconditional Love, we enjoy liberation not only from the pain of separation from our Divine identity but also liberation from the pain of separation from our Divine heart, unconditional Love. However, while we remain asleep at the level of our biology, we continue, as we mentioned, to experience not only biological pain but also the psychological pain buried in the life of our cells.

Asleep to the experience of the life of our body as an inseparable expression of Life of Being, as a leaf of the tree of Divine Life, we remain unconscious of our body's essential nature. Continuing to experience muscle, organ, blood and bone as separate components of a separate, personal body, we continue to experience separate consciousness at the level of the body. This separate consciousness continues, inevitably, to create and perpetuate physical degeneration, disease, and, ultimately, death.

Just as a caterpillar can only be reborn as a butterfly when it relinquishes completely its caterpillar form, so, less visibly but just as radically, we only unfold Divine body of Life/Light when we surrender not only the experience of a separate mind and heart but also of a separate, finite body; allowing the whole of our separate, human individuality, mind, heart and body to metamorphose, like logs igniting into flame, into Divine Light/Love and immortal Life. During this ultimate metamorphosis of corruptible body into Divine body of Life/Light, the experience of the body becomes increasingly less particle, less matter, and more living wave of Divine Life. Moreover, just as the metamorphosis of separate identity into our one Divine identity and separate heart into Divine heart, is usually a gradual, organic process rather than an instant transformation, so, too, is the metamorphosis of corruptible biology into immortal body of Life/Light.

Whereas I can write from personal experience something about awakening and embodying Light/Love of Being, I can, with one exception, only write about the transformation of corruptible body into immortal body of Life/Light, the embodying of Life of Being, from intuition and revelation.

This one exception occurred about thirty years ago. I was lying in bed as the first rays of the sun were beginning to shine through the leaves of the tree outside my bedroom window. Suddenly I experienced my physical body dissolving into light. I was not leaving my body in some form of astral projection, but, instead, my whole biological, sense-perceptible body was transmuting into light. The experience lasted, perhaps, only a few seconds, but those few seconds were long enough to provide a tiny glimpse of what it means and feels like for the body to dematerialize, and unfold its true nature as light.

While direct experience is both more authentic and reliable than intuition and revelation, it feels appropriate to share my intuition and revelation about the potential metamorphosis of our biology. Since such sharing by any of us may contribute to our understanding of the relationship between consciousness (including unconsciousness) and health. It may contribute to our realization that who we have been conditioned to believe we are, including biologically, is not who we truly are and, thereby, quicken the unfolding of our

177

true nature, not just Divine mind and heart but also Divine body.

A common argument leveled against the unfolding of Divine body of Life/Light is that our individual bodies, like Earth's body, are inevitably subject to natural rhythms of birth and death. However, this is only true of bodies reflective of separate consciousness. The essential nature of who we are, Light of Being, Divine Self, is not characterized by inevitable "natural" rhythms of life and death. It is immortal, unchanging and eternal. Just as heart of Being is not subject to the polarity of likes and dislikes, love and fear, Life of Being is not subject to the polarity of life and death.

It is only relative, separate consciousness that tells us our bodies are solid, finished, imperfect things that we can tinker with, enhancing their relative health, but never completely healing them into absolute health - wholeness. Only our conditioning that programs us to believe our bodies are condemned by their very nature to the inevitable pain of degeneration, disease and death.

After living for so long within this conditioning, this belief and experience of separation and duality, most of us have forgotten that this virtual reality is simply a reflection of our consciousness. Not our true reality; not who we are.

We have forgotten that health and wholeness, at every level of experience, is, in reality, who we are. Forgotten that, just as our Divine mind and heart are eternally untouched by mental and emotional ignorance, conflict, lack, suffering and pain, Divine body of Life/Light is similarly eternally untouched by the drama of degeneration and death.

When we believe that health depends, at least to some degree, on so-called "outside" energies and substances, we communicate to our cells that health is something we have to maintain or restore. We tell our body that health is not our natural, unconditional state, but, on the contrary, conditional on substances, genetics, exercise etc. We, thereby, perpetuate a biological experience that is, indeed, dependent for its relative and, ultimately, ephemeral health on seemingly "outside" substances and practices. For, as the new biology knows, everything we say, think, imagine, feel and believe is registered by our bodies, and reflected by molecular change.[29] Not only everything we consciously think, imagine, feel and believe, the tip of our consciousness iceberg, but also everything we unconsciously think, imagine, feel and believe – the much greater unconscious part of the iceberg.

When Jesus said "I and the father are one", (*John 10:30*), he acknowledged his realization of Oneness, the realization that there is only one of us, Divine consciousness expressing as all that is. When, by way of what the New Testament refers to as the transfiguration, resurrection and ascension, he realized Divine body of Life/Light, he revealed the whole nature of the Divine human.

Hans Heltoft, a Danish author, offers an inspiring picture of the ascended Jesus is his account of his experience in a Gestapo prison during World War II.

"Five hundred prisoners of various nationalities were occupied with weaving mats in a damp and moldy cellar. A guard entered and beat a Russian to death for no reason at all, pummeling the

---

[29] See *The Biology of Belief* by Bruce Lipton, and *You are the Placebo* by Dr. Joe Dispenza for the new science of the mind/body relationship.

lifeless, bleeding remains again and again. We prisoners felt every blow on our own bodies... One Polish prisoner, at his wit's end, called out: "That's enough." We all repeated in muffled voices: "That's enough." At that moment Jesus entered the cellar. I do not belong to the Church and I had never seen Jesus before. And yet I did know him, and I noticed that the others recognized him... His entire appearance transcended our normal conception of things. The only thing that is clear to me today is that this Jesus was Something Indescribable – and yet at the same time a normal human being. And although I am not a member of the Church I must say: This was the Greatest that we had ever experienced and ever will be able to experience. Simultaneously with Jesus' entrance, the following took place: the damp and moldy room became completely transformed... bright red and blue shades of color permeated the room and a sphere spread out which gave one a feeling of peace... The space up to the ceiling appeared to be so vast that one could have built a great barn in it... Jesus did not look at us... He contemplated the mutilated person lying at his feet. His face radiated love – a love which cannot be expressed in words... He bent over the Russian and gently kissed him on his bloody, swollen cheek. The man, whom we had considered dead, opened one eye. The other was ... closed with blood. When he saw Jesus, his mistreated face shone with childlike joy. With great difficulty he stretched out one hand toward Jesus. Jesus, bending over a little, took it in both his hands.

It was so indescribably beautiful that we all stood there smiling silently – also the guard. The Russian sank down, and the unmentionably beautiful expression which had settled upon the disgracefully abused figure disappeared. Jesus gently laid the

Russian's hand back upon his body and left the cellar. Immediately everything was as it had been before."[30]

In the initiation symbolized by the transfiguration of Jesus, separate consciousness is permeated, infused and enlightened by our Divine nature, Light of Being; metamorphosing personal mind, heart and biology, reflective of separate consciousness, into Divine mind, heart and body. In the initiation, symbolized by the crucifixion, the transfiguration is completed. The human body, reflective of separate consciousness, dies. The energy signature of the new human body, reflective of Divine I Am consciousness, is given to our greater body, the Earth, thereby seeding the potential for the body of the Earth and all human bodies to metamorphose into Divine body of Life/Light.

In the initiation symbolized by the resurrection and ascension of Jesus the human body completes its metamorphosis from mortal, biological body into an ethereal, immortal body of Life/Light, capable, when necessary, of condensing into a subtle, though visible, human form and dematerializing back into Light/Life of Being.

Once the metamorphosis of emotional body into Divine heart of unconditional Love is well underway, River of Light/Love/Life drops down into our biology. Our biological metamorphosis occurs in the same way as the metamorphosis of personal heart into Divine heart. As we embrace into the hearth of our heart each experience of physical discomfort, our cellular reflections of our psychological wounds, the Divine flame of Love ignites these unwhole energies,

---

[30] This account of Christ is given in Hans-Werner Schroeder's book *Von der Wiederkunft Christi heute* ("*The Reappearance of Christ in Our Time*").

reflective of separate consciousness, back into wholeness, into Love. It ignites this densest expression of separate consciousness until our corruptible body, relaxing out of pain and conflict into alignment with the Divine human blueprint, metamorphoses into immortal body of Life/Light.

As our biological metamorphosis begins, we awake to the body as naturally self-sustaining, self-generating and eternally whole. We realize that, just as our true heart is the complete, unconditional Love that we used to look to others to provide, our body is the absolute health we used to search for from food, supplements, sleep, exercise and pharmaceuticals.

The metamorphosis of physical body into ethereal body of Life/Light unfolds safely provided we remain fully in our body and allow, rather than force, River of Light/Love/Life to permeate our cells. In time, we notice our experience of physical, sense-perceptible body beginning to refine and enlighten; and, ultimately, to transform into immortal body of Life/Light.

During this transformational experience, we are respectful, sensitive to and discerning of the body's messages. Trusting it knows exactly what it needs at each stage of its metamorphosis from matter into Light/Life, we continue to provide it food and water for as long as it seems to need these. We rest it for as long as it experiences tiredness.

In the early passages of biological metamorphosis, our vitality and health may not seem to change much, if at all. It may even seem to deteriorate. We may experience a wide variety of physical symptoms, flu-like feelings, tiredness and other experiences of dis-ease, as the body relinquishes discordant, toxic, denser energies, and aligns with the subtler harmonious energies of our true nature, Light/Love/Life of Being.

Even when there are no overt physical challenges, the experience of biological metamorphosis may still feel intense. For as the subtler and more powerful energies of Light course through our body, refining and transforming our body experience, it may feel as though our body is plugged into an electric socket. It is - a Divine energy socket. So, during this transformational experience, we are respectful, sensitive to and discerning of the body's messages. Trusting it knows exactly what it needs at each stage of its metamorphosis from matter into Light/Life, we continue to provide it food and water for as long as it seems to need these. We rest it for as long as it experiences tiredness.

Moreover, we remain vigilant around any attempt by separate ego consciousness to resurrect itself and coopt the metamorphosis of the body into its own service. For, while the will of Divine Self assures a benevolent and harmonious transformation, the will of separate ego consciousness can result in spontaneous combustion rather than graceful metamorphosis.

If it feels difficult to discern whether the transformation of the body is leading to biological death or metamorphosis, or the process is feeling uncomfortable and intense, it can be useful to ground more fully into our greater body, the Earth; allowing a deeper experience of her sustaining presence. Also, to remain vigilant around any residual emotional attachment to a particular outcome. Moreover, as with each passage of our unfolding, it is always helpful to ask for guidance and support from Divine Self, as well as from those benevolent beings ready to facilitate our unfolding.

As the residual signatures of separate consciousness, carried in and as our cells, dissolve, our experience of biological pain diminishes. Instead of feeling contracted and discordant, each member of the biological community, each biological system and organ begins to reveal its unique energetic tone within the symphony that is Divine body. While the energy tone of the subtle life of limbs, for example, feels different from the tone of the subtle life of our heart or head, each tone feels exquisite and harmonious with every other tone.

Our incorruptible body, our perfect, immortal body of Life/Light is the body described in the Gospel of Philip as the true flesh:

"The (Lord rose) from the dead. (He became as he used to be, but now (his body) was perfect. He did indeed possess flesh, but this (flesh is) true flesh. (Our flesh) is not true. We possess only an image of the true."[31]

Jesus emphasizes in the Gospels that the only difference between him and us is that he is awake as Light of I Am, while most of us still sleep to our Divine nature. Instead of worshipping a Divine Jesus figure as someone special and separate from us, Jesus invites us to awake as the one Light of I Am, the Christ consciousness that he embodied during the last few years of his earthly life. He invites us to recognize that, as we relinquish the experience of separation and wholly

---

[31] *The Rainbow Body of Light*, William Henry, Arcanum, April 2014 Gaiatv

embody Light/Love/Life of Being, we too will spontaneously unfold Divine immortal body of Life/Light.

During the eons of inhabiting separate consciousness we forgot we are here on Earth not only to awake as Light/Love/Life of Being but also to embody Light/Love/Life of Being at every level of human experience. We forgot that the body, as condensed Light/Love/Life of Being, is no less Divine than heart and mind, and, as Divine life, is synonymous with health, vitality, harmony and immortal Life. We forgot that our true body, like our true mind and heart, is not limited by the experience of space/time, but, instead, limitless: transcendent, beyond all dimensions, and simultaneously capable of expressing in all dimensions, all densities of experience.

Even for those of us who, at this moment, may not feel called into the chrysalis of biological metamorphosis, the recognition of the Divine nature of the body, nevertheless, gifts us. For awareness of the body as condensation of who we are, Light of Being, profoundly enhances our respect for the one Divine being expressing as our individual body. It enhances our receptivity to the body's communications, to its subtlest signals of health and discomfort. Moreover, it encourages a deeper listening to, discerning and honoring of the body's innate Divine intelligence and guidance – our bone wisdom, our gut knowing.

Just as the caterpillar does not transform into a butterfly by elevating itself above its caterpillar body, we humans do not unfold the Divine nature of the body by elevating awareness above body and Earth. While the natural unfolding of Divine body of Life/Light is an ascension of consciousness, an ascension from separate consciousness into Divine

185

consciousness, it is an ascension, like the ascension of personal heart into Divine heart, that can only unfold by way of the descension of consciousness into the densest realms of mind, heart and, ultimately, body.

As each of us embodies and unfolds more of who we are, our awakening consciousness shines into humanity's collective consciousness, unveiling, transforming and enlightening our collective ignorance and darkness. In place of the mental, emotional and biological pain and suffering of separate consciousness, our Divine nature, embodying in each of us as River of Light/Love/Life unfolds the Divine wellbeing and harmony that defines the new human, the new humanity.

Meditative Play: Unfolding immortal body of Light

Summary of Passage 9

Just as Divine Light of Being metamorphoses personal mind and heart, reflective of separate consciousness, into Divine mind and heart, so too, like the caterpillar in the chrysalis, the complete embodiment of Divine Light of Being not only in the mind and heart, but also the body, metamorphoses our personal, corruptible body, reflective of separate consciousness, into Divine body/immortal body of Light/Life, thereby completing the unfolding the new Divine human.

As you play with this practice, if it feels appropriate, ask Divine Self and your spirit guides to facilitate and illuminate your experience.

1. With awareness above your crown, relax into the silence between thoughts, images, emotions and sensations.

2. Surrender any separate identity, and awake as Light of Being.

3. Rest as Light of I AM.

4. Allow Light of Being, as River of Light, to flow down the spine, expressing through the heart center as unconditional Love.

5. Rest as heart of Being, heart of all that is, Divine intelligent, unconditional Love.

6. Allow Light of Being to flow on down the spine, expressing through pelvis and root center as immortal Life.

7. Rest as Life of our greater Body, the Earth and all Life everywhere.

8. With awareness in the heart, unconditionally accept each physical sensation into the hearth of the heart, allowing flame of Being to ignite each physical sensation, each energy signature of separate consciousness back into our One Divine Self – Light/Love/Life of Being .

9. Experience Light of Being refining, purifying and enlightening each cell of the body, allowing the relative density of the sense perceptible body to metamorphose into Divine body/ immortal body of Life/Light.

PASSAGE 10

Being the New Human

"I searched for God and found only myself. I searched for myself and found only God."

Jalaluddin Rumi

Verily I say unto you, Inasmuch as ye have done it unto one of the least of these my brethren, ye have done it unto me."

Matthew 25:40 King James Bible

As we have seen, our sleeping human consciousness experiences itself as separate from all that is, separate from Source. Our awakening human consciousness experiences Self as Oneness, as one Light/Love/Life of Being expressing as all existence. Our sleeping consciousness, defined by separation and, therefore, suffering, experiences life as a struggle for survival, a struggle to fulfill physical, emotional, mental and spiritual needs from outside of who we experience our self to be. Our awakening consciousness experiences nothing existing outside of Self, for awakening as Divine being is awakening as one ocean of Being, as absolute wholeness and, therefore absolute fulfillment expressing as limitless, unique waves of experience.

189

Awakening as the benevolent whole that includes all experience while identifying with none, the new human awakens as the absolute perfection and limitless potential of Being. She/he awakens as Divine pristine Being expressing as all that is, while untouched by any and all expressions. Awakening as Light, Love and Life of Being, and experiencing Light, Love and Life as different experiences of Being and, simultaneously, different consciousness passages into Being, she is Divine Being spontaneously unveiling its Self to its Self.[32]

Neither separate consciousness nor awakening consciousness are single levels of consciousness, but, instead, different levels of the spectrum of consciousness. For example, one level of separate consciousness is when we wholly identify with and are wholly preoccupied with our experience of our self as a personal, separate "I", together with all the struggle, pain and suffering this inevitably implies. Honoring personal will over the will of others and the will of the Divine, we live wholly in service to our separate "I". Compelled by desires and fears, by the pain reflective of our experience of separation, we live in conflict with our essential nature and, therefore, in conflict with all life.

A more evolved level of separate consciousness is when we attempt to balance service to personal self with service to others. When we attempt to be both considerate to ourselves and to others; to honor and appreciate our personal self as well as all living beings, visible and invisible.

A still more evolved level of separate consciousness is one in which, while still sleeping to our Divine nature, we,

---

[32] For the rest of this passage, I use "she" to designate both "he" and "she".

nevertheless, honor the Divine; and, inspired by devotion to the Divine, dedicate our lives to serving all life everywhere. We contribute what we can to birthing a more benevolent, harmonious and compassionate world. Whether through prayer, loving intention, and/or humanitarian work, we walk lightly on the Earth, with gratitude for all that she is and all that she gives; sharing what we have and caring for all life everywhere.

The spectrum of awakening consciousness, the spectrum of the new human consciousness, begins when we recognize or intuit the truth of our Divine nature, Light/Love/Life of Being expressing as all existence, even while we still sleep to a conscious experience of this nature. Inspired by the recognition of who we are, we dedicate our lives to awakening out of the sleep of separation; awakening as changeless Divine Presence expressing as all change.

At higher levels of the spectrum of awakening consciousness are the enlightening humans - those who, awakening as Divine consciousness, are also unfolding Divine intelligent, unconditional Love and, ultimately, Divine immortal body of Life/Light. Some, like Jesus and others so wholly embody our Divine nature that they can not only master the elements but also, when it is the highest good, elevate all life into Divine wholeness and health.

The consciousness of separation, responsible for thousands of years of human conflict and fear, litigates social and cultural laws to minimize the inevitable chaos and pain inherent in the experience of separation. It litigates human relating, such as divorce and child custody, in the attempt to limit the conflict and suffering inherent in our disconnection from unconditional Love, and, thereby, promote the wellbeing of children.

Our current legislation of human relating reflects the perspective of separate consciousness that each human heart is separate from every other human heart, and, therefore, fundamentally in service to itself rather than in service to the whole. It reflects the belief of separate consciousness that we need governments and legal systems to control our social and moral choices, because, without such control, our inherently selfish nature would inevitably birth chaos, neglect, conflict and cruelty.

There is truth to this perspective of separate consciousness. It seems we need certain social and cultural regulations to corral and minimize the chaos, conflict, exploitation, greed and cruelty that we birth when we sleep to the experience of all living beings as our Self. We need the protection of some laws while we sleep to the heart of who we are - while we sleep to Love.

However, as we awake out of separate consciousness into the one heart of Being, we gradually cease to need laws or even cultural traditions to control our relating. For now, instead of being run ragged by our sleeping heart, compelled by emotional hunger and pain into the creation of more pain, we are awakening as the absolute fulfillment, wholeness and wellbeing of our one heart - Divine intelligent, unconditional Love. Not only hearing the guidance of Love but increasingly honoring this guidance, we live in service to the highest good for all, rather than in service to a lonely, hungry, separate self.

As our sensitivity to the will and heart of Being refines and unfolds, we know spontaneously when and how to relate to each other, when and how to cherish and support each other - how to love our children, friends and aging relatives. We no longer need to legislate consideration and caring for each other and the Earth. While we may continue to create social agreements about some practical things, like which side of the road to drive on, we no longer need to legislate caring through welfare programs. We no longer need laws to protect us from our disconnection from Love expressing as theft, greed, racism, sexism and violence. The Love that we are embraces a sick stranger, the violence in a distant country and political dissent in our own. Awake as One Being, experiencing the other as our Self, we spontaneously relate to the other as our Self, and we naturally honor and celebrate the other's unique expression of Being, just as we honor and celebrate our own.

Similarly, as we awake as Love, we no longer need to circumscribe our intimate relating with social, cultural and legal constraints. Whereas social, cultural and legal constraints impose general patterns of intimate relating on us, only Love knows what is right for each of us, individually and collectively, in each situation. Only Love knows who needs to come together in intimacy, which man and woman, which man and man, or woman and woman. Only Love knows when it is right to enter or leave a relationship; and only Love knows what kind of relationship. While monogamy, for example, may be the will of Love for some of us during certain passages of our unfolding, and therefore our highest good, during other passages monogamy may stifle our unfolding consciousness, and therefore oppose the will of Love.

As we transition from human relating defined and controlled by social, cultural and political constraints to human relating reflecting the will of Divine, intelligent, unconditional Love we need, as always, discernment. We need, for example, the ability to discern between our awakening Divine heart and the residues of our separate, emotional heart eager to co-opt the language of awakening in service to its gnawing hunger or fear of authority, both human and Divine. We need the ability to discern whether we are truly hearing the guidance of Love and, therefore, no longer need the safeguards of political, social and religious laws, or whether we think, imagine or hope we are hearing the guidance of Love, and, therefore, still need these safeguards. Whenever we are living from separate consciousness, searching for Love from others rather than experiencing Love as who we are, we probably continue to need some social and cultural constraints.

Gradually, as a critical number of us humans awake out of the sleep of separation and suffering, and hear the Divine guidance of the heart, outer authorities will become redundant. Increasingly, our actions, words, feelings and creations, every facet of our life, will spring spontaneously from our true nature, Light/Love/Life of Being. The life of each of us will inevitably enhance the lives of all of us. Living as unique, unfolding embodiments of our one Divine Self, we will live in harmony with each other and all life everywhere; spontaneously unfolding and expressing the way of Love, the highest good for all existence.

Many years ago, while visiting Australia, I experienced something of what it means for the patterns of intimate relating to be guided by the will of Love rather than the customs and laws of western society. I was walking up a steep sidewalk in a small town in Eastern Australia with an

194

Australian friend, Peter. Just before the local health food store, we met a tall, thin man with wild, auburn, curly hair, white skin, armbands and strong, bare feet. To my European eyes, he looked like a mix of a Scottish baron and an indigenous Australian. He was accompanied by two exuberant young children and their mother. Peter introduced me to this unusual looking man as his Shamanic teacher. He called him Jaru, which I later discovered was just one of his many names since indigenous Australians assume the name expressive of each significant relationship, rather than a name signifying their individual self.

After a few seconds adjusting to Jaru's strange appearance, our eyes met over the unbrushed heads of his young children. It was one of those "eyes across the room" moments. I was instantly aware of a profound and ancient bond between this barefooted, wild man and myself.

We did not speak to each other in that first meeting on the sidewalk; not even a word of greeting. We simply experienced the harmonious presence flowing between and as us while Peter talked with Merilli, the mother of the children, and the little ones played around. Then the youngest child, who was just learning to walk, fell and cut her leg. Jaru immediately rolled her over onto her stomach and lay her flat on the sidewalk. I watched, wondering at first why this strange and yet intensely familiar man did not pick up his daughter and comfort her in his arms. Then I realized he was giving her first to our primary mother, the Earth, for comfort and healing. I watched with discomfort as she lay crying on the cold, hard sidewalk, but restrained myself from going over to her and giving her the comfort that it seemed, according to my western values, she needed. I watched as she continued to bleed and cry. I watched and waited until, after a minute or two that felt much longer, she relaxed and stopped crying. Only then did Merilli pick her up and comfort her, adding her caring to what her daughter had received from the Earth. Relieved to see the little one in her mother's arms, my eyes returned to the eyes of her father, and the compelling harmony of our hearts.

The following afternoon Peter and I visited Jaru and his family. As soon as I walked into his house, Jaru led me back out of the dark living room into the intense Australian sun. For about an hour we stood facing each other on the grass outside his front door. Again our meeting was largely silent. Words seemed unnecessary, except when I asked him for some water, and when he reassured me that the love we were experiencing together; could not in any way violate his relationship with Merilli.

While my entrenched Western values around monogamy were not reassured by his words, a deeper part of my heart trusted what was unfolding between us. The energy felt clean; different from familiar romantic attraction with its attendant emotional fantasies and compulsions. I felt no energetic stickiness in either of us; no emotional hunger for more. No busy thoughts about the significance of our connection; what it might or might not lead to. Instead, our hearts, awake in that moment as unconditional Love, were simply experiencing each other as Love.

I felt we were reawakening to a union between us that had always been there. A union that I had forgotten growing up the other side of the Earth, in England, as a member of the culture that had committed unspeakable atrocities, including genocide, on Jaru's people. In a memory flash, I saw myself

196

as a young child digging into the English mud with a toy spade to see if I could dig all the way down through the Earth until I came to the land on the other side of the world, known in English as Australia. (The name 'Australia' was given to this land by the Europeans. Indigenous people speak of it in other ways).

Silently and without touching, as we continued to stand in the searing sun outside Jaru's front door, our hearts continued to open deeper into Love. When it is was time for Peter and I to leave, I simply looked into the eyes of my new friend, thanked him and walked away. We said nothing to each other about meeting again. It seemed there was nothing to be said. Our meeting felt whole. I felt no emotional hunger compelling me to suggest another meeting. Just Love.

A few days later, having said goodbye to Peter, I was standing in my motel room contemplating whether to travel south to Byron Bay, when I felt Jaru's energetic presence beside me. Surprised by the almost palpable experience of him, I reached for my phone and called him. I told him I was preparing to move on, and thanked him for our time together.

"Are you complete with this area?" he asked me. "The only thing that feels incomplete", I heard myself saying "is our connection".

So we arranged to meet later that afternoon.

As we sat on the grass together in a secluded wooded area, my heart knew I would not be going to Byron Bay. It was clear I had crossed the Pacific Ocean to be with Jaru.

A few days later he and I talked to Merilli and received her blessing for Jaru and I to venture into deeper intimacy with each other. Jaru had already explained to me that he and Merilli lived in accordance with traditional indigenous values, and that these included the possibility of either partner having more than one intimate "mate" when this felt "right" for the whole family. He also explained that intimate relationships among his people were regarded as very sacred. Not to be entered lightly, but only when both people's hearts, rather than their emotional bodies, felt an unquestionable sense of rightness.

During our three-way conversation, Merilli confirmed what Jaru had already said. She acknowledged that from the beginning of their relationship she had accepted that, should either of them meet someone else whom they also experienced as a life partner, they would welcome that person into their life. Jaru later told me that, soon after he and I met, Merilli had mentioned to him that she felt he and I belonged together as part of their extended family.

Jaru further explained that what he meant by "rightness" is fundamentally different from western ideas and experiences of romantic attraction, based as they often are on ephemeral fantasies, emotional hunger and projection onto the other of qualities we humans can only, ultimately, unfold within. He explained that the indigenous meaning of "rightness" refers to the spiritual destiny of the two people to be in intimate relationship together, regardless of whether such a relationship feels emotionally comfortable or uncomfortable to those involved. He said that this "rightness" is recognized as an expression of a higher will, rather than the will of personal ego, and, is, therefore, accepted and honored, regardless of any practical or emotional complications it might generate.

He acknowledged that these days including more than one intimate relationship within a family may trigger into consciousness hitherto unacknowledged and unhealed "stuff" since many of us have lived lifetimes of disconnection from the Love that we are, and have, thereby, accumulated layers of hunger and wounding.

Initially, I found the idea of becoming part of a polyamorous family uncomfortable, to say the least. While my heart and every bone of my body seemed to experience a knowing that Jaru and I were destined to be together, my surface, culturally conditioned, mind balked at the idea. Unhealed emotional wounds within me were instantly triggered by the possibility of embarking on an intimate relationship with a man already involved with another woman. I felt an immediate temptation to protect myself from experiencing these wounds by walking away from such a complicated, emotionally triggering situation. I also felt protective of Merilli's emotions. I knew that, if Jaru and I became lovers, it would trigger every residue of emotional rejection, abandonment and jealousy not only in me but also in her. Moreover, I felt concern for young children. How would it be for them to see their father making love with me in their home? For Jaru had made it clear that our loving, if we chose to go that way, would not be hidden from the children, but, instead, openly welcomed and celebrated by the whole family.

Then there were the geographical issues. I felt little resonance with this raw, strong land. I appreciated its wild power, but my body missed the subtle, soft, vitality of Hawaii, that had been my home for many years. So how and why, my mind asked, should I embark on an intimate relationship with this strange man and his large family in this unfamiliar, wildland? Yet, alongside all these seemingly valid questions, concerns and reservations, the still, deep voice of the heart seemed to continue to invite me to accept Jaru's invitation to be his "mate". Beside the power of this quiet voice, my questions, fears, reservations and concerns felt like flotsam on the ocean of Being. Present, yes, but unquestionably not the voice of Love.

During the first few weeks and months of our intimacy together, sometimes in his family house and sometimes in my motel, I felt thrust into a wild, raw world, bereft of emotional, mental, cultural and human support. Amidst days and nights of loving, rooted in our mutual sense of the rightness of being together, our mutual experience of being the Love we shared, my mind, emotions and nervous system were shocked out of old beliefs, attitudes, behaviors and emotional comfort zones.

As I experienced Jaru moving between me and Merilli, the children's natural embrace of me as another "mother"; and Merilli's acceptance of me into their family, I felt stripped of emotional patterns, preferences and attachments that I had carried for years - maybe lifetimes. I experienced layers of hitherto unknown, and therefore unhealed emotional wounds erupting painfully into consciousness; and being transformed through awareness and acceptance into Love. This raw, rapid and sometimes shocking energy transformation eroded many of my culturally conditioned intimacy patterns. My heart felt progressively stripped of expectations and assumptions around how Love lives. This stripping of habitual, conditioned thoughts, beliefs and emotional junk unveiled more and more of the unconditioned, pristine nature of the heart; incrementally stabilizing the experience of being Love, relating as Love and walking the ways of Love, however unfamiliar these appeared and felt.

Apart from the poignancy of the large ocean that, much of the time, divided our physical bodies, Jaru and I rarely experienced ourselves in a long-distance relationship. Inasmuch as we were awake as Light/Love of Being, we did not experience any separation between us or between us and the ocean dividing our bodies. Instead we experienced the eternal ecstasy of the one Love, one Being that we are shining as two bodies, two lives in two lands. One heart unfolding, revealing and expressing its Self through two humans, eternally one. The same one Divine heart of unconditional Love present in our individual meditations and life walk, and yet also mysteriously different; somehow richer when consciously experienced between and as us.

While we missed enormously our physical closeness and the joy of sharing our lives in body on the Earth, our energetic relating unfolded subtler levels of being and relating than we might have consciously experienced if we had always been able to live on the same piece of Earth. We became increasingly sensitive to each other's energetic presence, immediately recognizing when we were energetically present with each other.

Mostly communicating energetically rather than verbally, we began to feel more strongly the creative power of each other's thoughts and feelings. Unable to smell the scent of each other's physical skin, we began to awake to the subtler scents and touch of each other's etheric, life force bodies. Often I could "feel" the strands of Jaru's curly hair "touching" my face, or the "caress" of his etheric lips. Many nights I went

201

to sleep feeling his energetic body lovingly wrapped around me, subtly tangible, just less so than his physical body.

While our absolute reality is always and only Divine consciousness, Oneness, the new human awakes as unity consciousness and, simultaneously, as relative, multidimensional consciousness. She can, for example, enjoy sense-perceptible, physical loving. She can also enjoy subtle energy loving. She can relate to another with her physical senses in space/time consciousness and, when geographically separated, she can relate at levels of consciousness unbound by space/time. Sitting with a friend under an old oak tree, she can appreciate the unique individuality of herself and her friend as well as the spirit presence of the oak tree. She can also appreciate the elemental and ancestral spirits surrounding herself, her friend and the oak tree.

Awakening as Light of Being, the new human is awake not only as an individual human on our greater body, the Earth, but also as a member of group energy beings, soul, galactic and cosmic, and, simultaneously, as the one Light of Being expressing as each individual and group being. She is awake as Light of Being materializing and dematerializing; awake to all life everywhere, at every level of consciousness, as her Self.

While separate consciousness experiences relative freedom, awakening consciousness experiences absolute freedom. Separate consciousness experiences freedom as "freedom from", the freedom to do what it chooses, when it chooses and how it chooses, whereas absolute Divine freedom does not come and go. It is not born by a personal will experiencing itself as independent of other people, laws or situations; not something we can attain one day and lose the next. Not something that can be destroyed by prison bars. Absolute Divine freedom is who we are; paradoxically synonymous with Divine will.

As the new human awakes as and lives Divine will, rather than personal will, she may not, initially, understand Divine will. She may not comprehend the ways it births and unfolds individual, collective and Earth life. She may even be painfully triggered by how It unveils her psychological and biological residues of separate consciousness. However, she trusts and honors its ways. Instead of allowing separate consciousness to chart her life path, she allows Divine will, like the currents of the ocean, to move the wave of her life.

Since Divine Love is always inclusive, the awakening heart of the new human births personal, social and economic ways of inclusiveness. Ways born from unity consciousness and, therefore, reflecting caring and compassion for all existence as our Self. Ways that respect people of all races, cultures, ages, sexes, gender identities and spiritual orientation. Since inherent in unity consciousness is the recognition that each of us, as in the story of the blind men encountering the elephant (see Passage 1), may be partially blind to who we are. We may confuse a limited experience of our Divine nature with the whole. Just as, for example, some of us may experience the sun as light, others as warmth, and still others as life, some of us may experience our Divine nature as Light, others as Divine Love, and still others as Divine Life. Unity consciousness recognizes that our different experiences of our one Divine nature unfold more of the tapestry of truth than any one person, culture or spiritual tradition may unfold alone. It recognizes that our differences, including our different perspectives, gift us all.

The new human, honoring diversity, embodies natural humility. She humbly acknowledges that, since each of us is a work or play in progress, our understanding and experience of our Divine nature, inevitably unfolds organically, like the petals of a flower; rather than arising into consciousness complete and whole.

Her humility allows her, among other things, to honor and treasure her questions, trusting that each question spontaneously attracts its answer. When she notices a question rising into consciousness, she neither relies on others for the answer nor uses her intellect to figure out the answer. Instead, she carries the question gently, trusting the answer will arrive when she is ready to hear it. However the answer finally arrives, whether through a dream, a revelation or realization, her consciousness, like the proverbial lightbulb, lights up as it arrives in awareness, announcing the presence of truth.

When I was a teenager, I was reminded of this natural way of unfolding truth without the recourse to the intellect when I was told to write a paper on "serendipity". Since, at that time, I didn't know what the word meant, let alone how to fill many single-spaced pages with a discussion of it, I first looked it up in the dictionary, and then struggled to think about its meaning from as many angles as my intellect could identify. After hours of mental gymnastics, late at night, mentally and physically depleted, I leaned back in my chair and gave my tired body a break from thinking. As soon as I relaxed and stopped thinking, my awareness spontaneously moved into the silence between thoughts. Awakening, momentarily, as the silence of Being, insights about the meaning and implications of "serendipity" spontaneously downloaded into consciousness. They flooded my mind from what seemed to be their source, the Light of silence. Elated by the serendipitous discovery that truth is not sourced from intellect or books, but lives, instead, around and in us as the silent radiance of Being, I began making notes for my paper on serendipity.

Awakening as Light/Love/Life of Being, new humans also raise their children differently. As they walk gratefully and lovingly on our greater body, the Earth, taking from the Earth only what they need and giving to her the Love that facilitates her own unfolding, they allow their children to awake to the Earth as our greater body. Their parenting and educating are primarily invitations to their children to remember their Divine nature. While recognizing their children may need help discovering how to care for their bodies and navigate space/time, the new humans understand children do not need to be taught who they are. Instead, the new human parents simply mirror our Divine nature to their children, knowing that this mirroring will spontaneously unfold the children's experience of their essential nature. They mirror the wellbeing, wholeness and equanimity that is who we are, thereby spontaneously unfolding their children's experience of wellbeing, wholeness and equanimity. They mirror respect, appreciation and caring for all existence, each unique expression of our Divine Being, thereby unfolding their children's respect, appreciation and caring for every living being. The life of the new human parents mirrors the creativity and play of our Divine nature, thereby, spontaneously unfolding their children's creativity and play. By unconditionally Loving and accepting their children as unique revelations of who we are, even when saying "no" to some of their behaviors, the new human parents unfold their children's ability to Love and accept all life, both themselves and others.

When and if it feels right, the new humans teach their children to read, write, master various technologies and academic disciplines, while, always acknowledging the interconnectedness of all truth – the indivisible One that we are that expresses, for example, as both the language of music and the laws of mathematics.

Awakening as Being, the new human no longer needs agendas and goals. She does not struggle to attain status, power and self-worth, nor to placate an inner judge. Instead, awake as Light of Being, her doing is a spontaneous, creative, playful and unique expression of who she is, Divine Being. Her heart recognizes and experiences right work that is, simultaneously, right play in right way and right time. No longer a separate ego-consciousness struggling for survival. No longer a human "doer". The new human is simply Divine Presence unfolding as new human BEING.

Even when she has only a few dollars in her bank account, and feels physically exhausted, the new human experiences the limitless abundance of our essential nature. While monitoring her financial and biological reserves, she trusts that, in time, her sense-perceptible experience will mirror her experience of the Divine abundance that we are; that, in time, Divine Being will embody in her human experience not only as Divine mind, heart and immortal body of Life/Light but also as ample resources for her Earthly existence.

Awakening as Love, the new human heart radiates compassion for all beings suffering the pain of separate consciousness. Compassion for those of us awakening as

Light of Being, but whose hearts, still veiled by psychological pain, experience the pain of disconnection from heart of Being, from Love. Compassion for those, awakening as Light/Love of Being, but whose bodies, reflecting separate consciousness, still sleep to our immortal body of Life/Light and, therefore, still experience the physical discomfort of degeneration and disease.

The new humans, as we have seen, are the old humans liberated from the straitjacket of separate consciousness. They are who we are when, surrendering separate consciousness, we relinquish our identification with who we are not. When we awake as Divine Being and all expressions and experiences of Being while defining ourselves by none. When, ultimately, we allow not only personal mind and heart but also personal body to metamorphose into Divine mind, heart and immortal body of Life/Light.

Just as the metamorphosis of the personal mind, heart and body into Divine mind, heart and immortal body of Life/Light unfolds the new human and the new humanity, so the new humanity facilitates the metamorphosis of humanity's greater body, the Earth, into a new Earth. An Earth reflective of Light/Love/Life of Being: a natural world reflecting the harmony, vitality, abundance of our Divine nature.

With all the noblest intentions separate consciousness may attempt to transform our social, political, economic and psychological ways to birth cultures more reflective of compassion and respect for each other and all life, including the Earth. However, ultimately, all these noblest intentions are, at best, injections of benevolence into a perspective of spirit and matter, mind and body imbued by conflict and untruth. A dualistic perspective that, blind to body, matter and Earth as condensations of the mind and heart of the One that we are, inevitably perpetuates conflict and pain at every level of human and Earthly experience.

Although some of us, at least for a while, may continue to regard the metamorphosis of personal mind, heart and body into Divine mind, heart and immortal body of Life/Light as ungrounded fantasy, our human metamorphosis is, ultimately, unstoppable. While its timing is up to each one of us, dependent on our choices in each moment, the Divine flame of Being will, ultimately, consume the ignorance and disease inherent in separate consciousness into its Divine Self. Within the hearth of our hearts, unconditional Love will consume our pain into Love. Light/Love/Life of Being will consume our old human nature, reflective of separate consciousness, and birth the Divine new human - whole not only in mind and heart but also in body.

Meditative Play: Being the New Human on a New Earth

Summary of Passage 10

The new human is the one embodying Divine Being, as River of Light/Love/Life, thereby allowing the metamorphosis of personal mind, heart and body, reflective of separate consciousness, into Divine mind, heart and body. Our current socio/economic/political/spiritual and environmental crises cannot be resolved by the separate consciousness that created them. Only unity consciousness can unfold a world free of fear, judgment, ignorance, disease, conflict, poverty; free not only of all suffering, but all mental, emotional and biological pain.

If it feels appropriate, invite Divine Self and your spirit guides to enhance, facilitate, unfold and illuminate your experience.

1. With awareness above the crown of your head, become aware of Light of Being, Divine Presence in between your thoughts.

2. Surrendering any separate identity, relax as Divine Presence, Light of Being.

3. Allow Light of Being to flow into your crown, metamorphosing personal mind into Divine mind.

4. Allow Light of Being to flow from your crown, down your spine into your heart center.

5. Allow your heart to shine Light of Being as unconditional Love.

6. Surrendering the experience of a separate heart, allow Light of Being to metamorphose your personal heart into our one Divine heart expressing as each unique human heart.

7. As heart of Being, as unconditional Love, accept and honor all cultural, racial, gender, personality and spiritual differences.

8. As Divine heart of Being, experience unconditional love for someone who tends to trigger you.

9. Allow Light/Love of Being to flow from your heart down your spine into your root center.

10. Allow your root center to experience Light/Love of Being as immortal Life of Being.

11. Experience Being Divine immortal Life expressing as all life everywhere, as all existence.

12. As Light/Love/Life of Being, allow your personal, mortal body to metamorphose into Divine Body/Body of immortal Life/Light.

13. As Divine consciousness, as Light/Love/Life of Being, experience your self as the new human **Being** on a new Earth.

Copyright: Sukie Colegrave 2020